William Cumming Peters

Peters' Sodality Hymn Book

William Cumming Peters

Peters' Sodality Hymn Book

ISBN/EAN: 9783337083922

Printed in Europe, USA, Canada, Australia, Japan

Cover: Foto ©Thomas Meinert / pixelio.de

More available books at **www.hansebooks.com**

PETERS'
Sodality Hymn Book.

---•◆•---

COMPILED AND ARRANGED BY THE

SISTERS OF NOTRE DAME,

CINCINNATI, OHIO.

---•◆•---

Boston: Published by OLIVER DITSON & CO., 451 Washington Street.

NEW YORK — CHAS. H. DITSON & CO., Successors to J. L. Peters.   CHICAGO: LYON & HEALY.   CINCINNATI: DOBMEYER & NEWHALL, Successors to Lee & Walker.   PHILADELPHIA: J. E. DITSON & CO.

Entered, according to Act of Congress, in the year 1872, by J. L. Peters, in the Office of the Librarian of Congress, at Washington.

Publisher's Notice.

THE SODALITY HYMN BOOK has been compiled with great care, and we feel confident that its own merits will insure its success.

Compiled, as it has been, in honor of the most Gracious Queen of Heaven, we trust it will be received by our friends with the same spirit, and with the same warmth, that has characterized the Sisters' efforts in its compilation. It has been for them a labor of love; and we send it forth under the patronage of "Mary, the Mistress of our Hearts," in the hope that its circulation will tend to further promote that love and respect which we all owe to the Mother of God.

We also desire to give credit to MR. WILLIAM DRESSLER for the assistance which he has given in the arrangement of the work, and for the original Mass and Hymns which he has contributed.

J. L. PETERS,
Publisher.

PETERS'
SODALITY HYMN BOOK,

COMPILED AND ARRANGED BY THE

SISTERS OF NOTRE DAME,

CINCINNATI, OHIO.

LAUDATE DOMINUM IN SANCTIS EJUS. Psalm 150.

May be sung before the "*Asperges me,*" before Mass.

GREGORIAN.

1. Laudáte Dóminum in Sánctis e-jus, laudáte éum in firmaménto vir-tú-tis e-jus.
2. Laudáte éum in vir-tútibus e-jus, laudáte éum secúndum multitúdinem magni-tudines e-jus.
3. Laudáte eum in só-no tú-bae, laudáte éum in psalterio, et cithara.
4. Laudáte éum in tym-páno et chó-ro, laudáte éum in chordis, et órgano.
5. Laudáte éum in cymba-lis benesonántibus, laudáte éum ir. cymbális jubilá-ti-o-nis, ómnis spiritus lau-det Dóminum.
6. Gloria Patri et Fi-lio, et Spi - - - ri-tui Sancto.
7. Sicut erat in prin-ci-pió, et nunc et semper et in saecula saecu-lo-rum, A-men.

OUR FATHER. Chant.

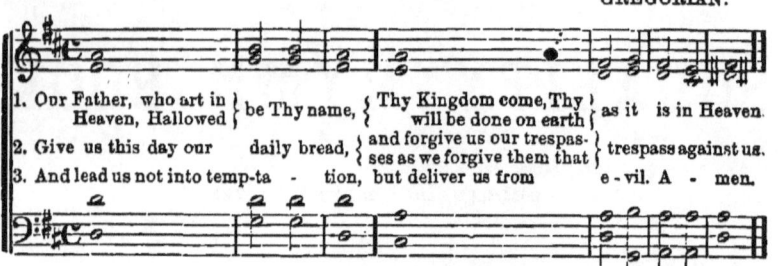

HAIL MARY. Chant.

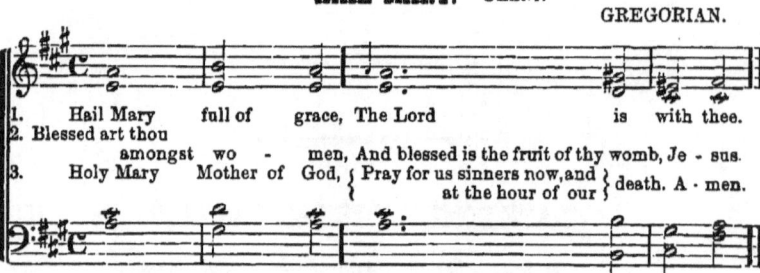

ACT OF CONTRITION. Chant.

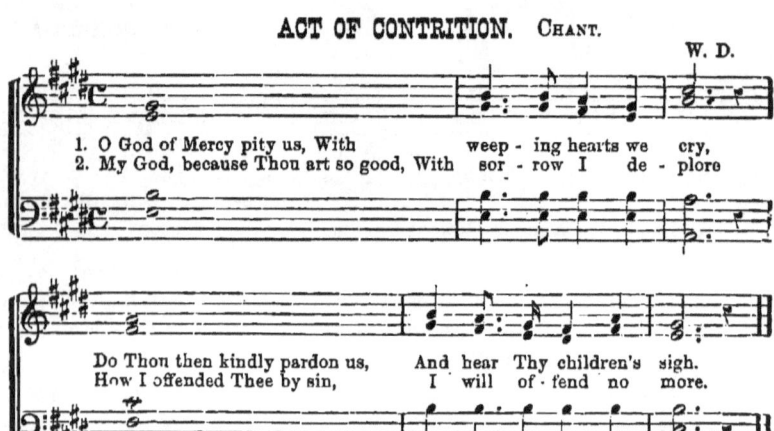

ASPERGES ME.

Sung before Mass, from Trinity to Palm Sunday inclusive.

2 VOICES & BASS AD LIB.

Repeat "*Vide Aquam*" to the Psalm "*Confitemini*,"
Versical and Responses the same as after the "*Asperges me*," page

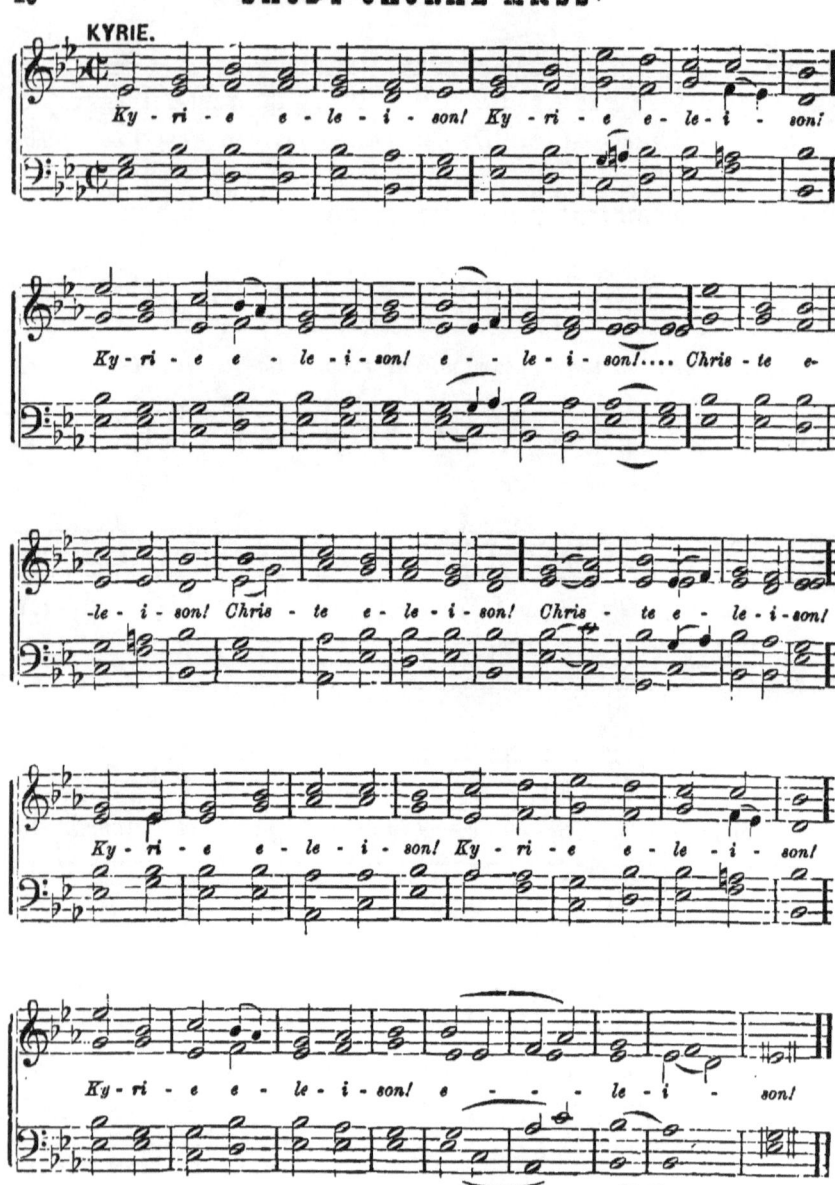

"Short Choral Mass." Continued.

"Short Choral Mass." Continued.

GLORIA, Continued.

"Short Choral Mass." Continued.

CREDO. The Priest intones, "*Credo in unum Deum.*"

"Short Choral Mass." Continued.

CREDO. Continued.

"Short Choral Mass." Continued.

O JESU, DEUS. For Offertory.

DUET. DRESSLER.

See pages 24, 25, 26, 65.

"Short Choral Mass." Continued.

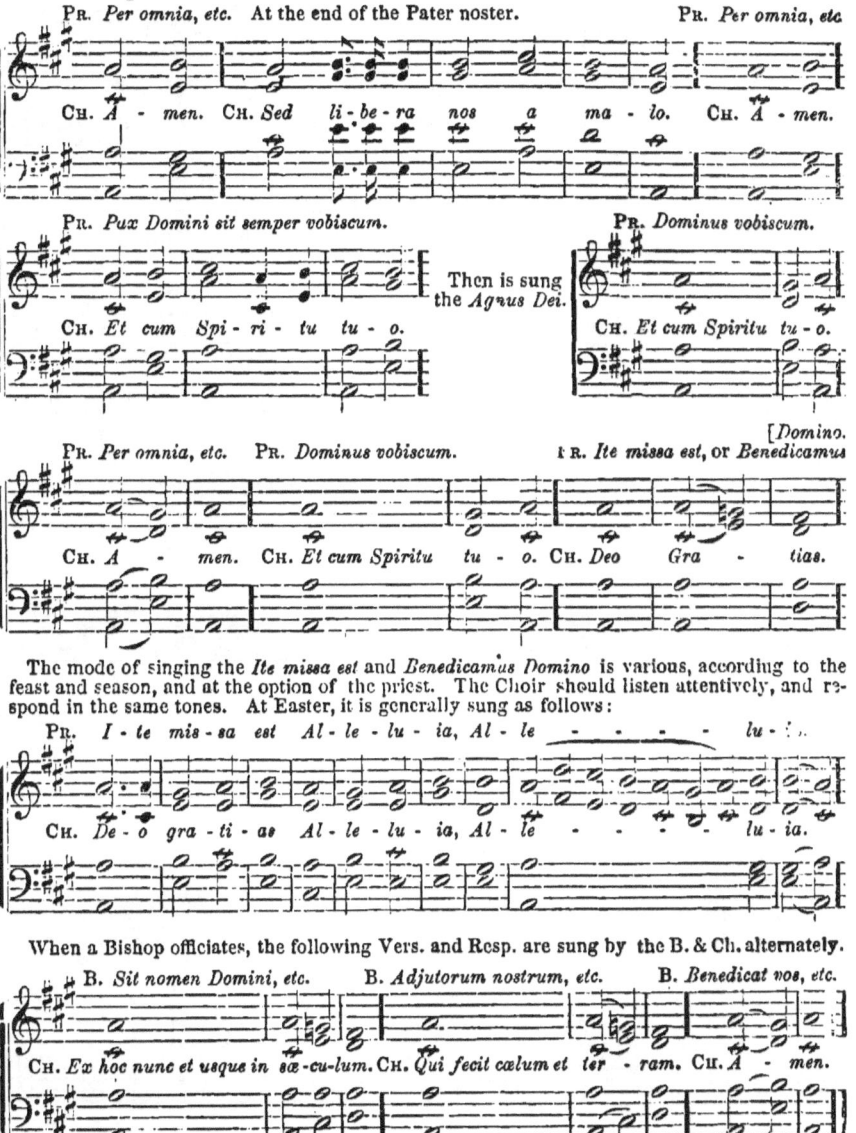

24. ADORO TE SUPPLEX. (Hymns for Offertory or Benediction.)
DUET OR TWO-PART CHORUS.

SHORT CHORAL REQUIEM MASS.

27

REQUIEM. W. Dressler.

Repeat Requiem to *Fine*, then pass immediately to the Kyrie.

"Requiem Mass." Continued. 29

There is no Gloria in the Mass for the Dead. Responses the same as in High Mass. Immediately after the Epistle comes the following:

DIES IRÆ.
Allegro moderato.

1. Di - es i - ræ di - es il - la, solvet sæclum in fa - vil - la
2. Quantus tre - mor est fu - tu - rus, quando Ju - dex est ven - tu - rus,

1 tes - te David cum Sy - bil - la.   3. Tu - ba mirum
2 cunc - ta stricte discus - su - rus.   4. Mors stu - pe - bit

3 spargens sonum per se - pulcra re - gi - o - num co - get omnes ante-
4 et na - tu - ra cum re - sur - get cre - a - tu - ra, ju - dicante respon-

3 -thro - num. 5. Li - ber scriptus pro - fe - re - tur, in quo
4 -su - ra.   6. Ju - dex er - go cum se - de - bit, quid quid

5 to - tum con - ti - ne - tur un - de mundus ju - di - ce - tur.
6 la - tet ad pa - re - bit, nil in - ultum re - man - de - bit.

"Requiem Mass." Continued.

Dies Iræ. Concluded.
Andante.

7 Re - cor - da - re Jesu pi - e quod sum cau-sa
9 La - cry - mo - sa di - es il - la, qua re - surget

tu - æ vi - tæ, ne me perdas il - la di - e.
ex fa - vil - la ju - di - candus ho - mo re - us.

8 Quæ-rens me se - dis - ti las-sus, re - de - mis - ti crucem passus·
10 Hu - ic er - go par - ce De - us Pi - e Je - su Do - mi - ne,

tan - tus labor non sit cas - sus. Do - na e - is Re - qui-
do - na e - is requi - em.

-em. A - men, A - - men.

There is no Credo.

"Requiem Mass." Continued.

DOMINE JESU CHRISTE. (Offertory.)

"Requiem Mass." Continued.

AGNUS DEI.

"Requiem Mass." Continued.

AGNUS DEI. Continued.

RESPONSES AFTER THE LIBERA. (Without Organ.) 37

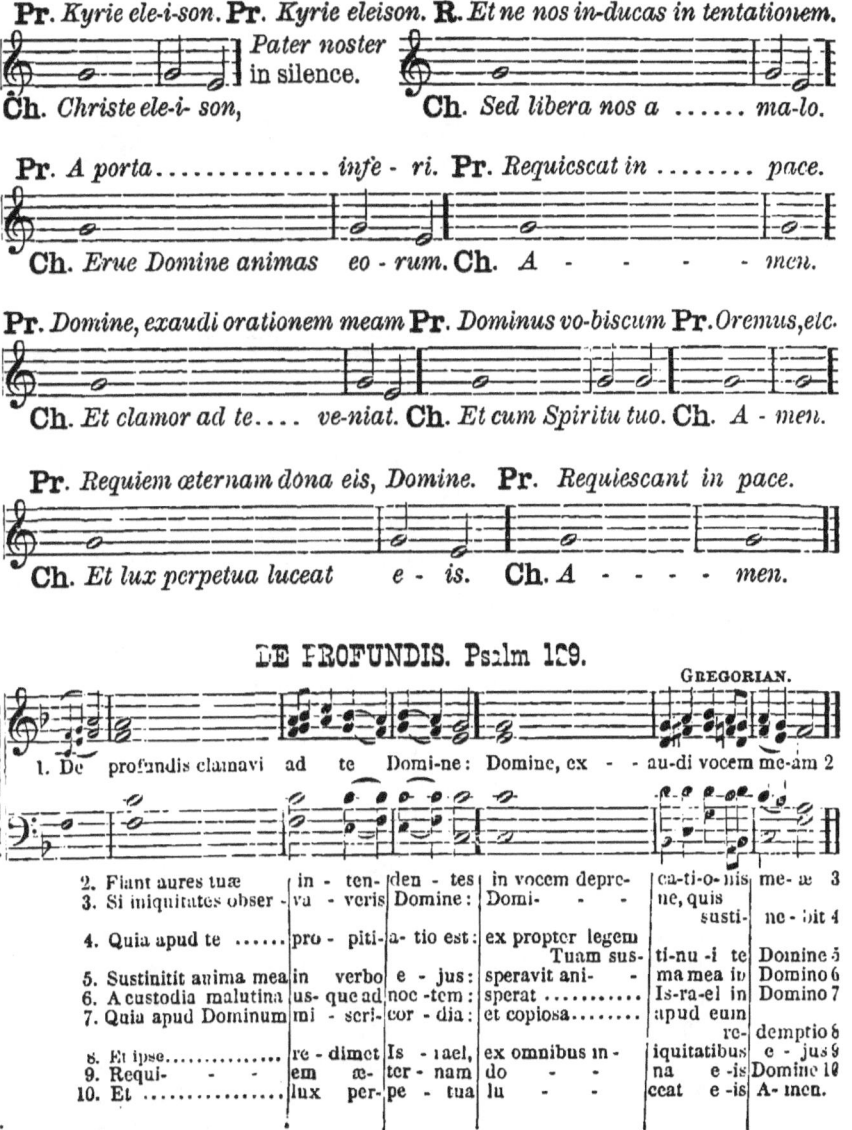

MISERERE. Psalm 50.

For Lent, Funerals and Penitential Occasions.

GREGORIAN.

1. Mi - - serere............ .... me - - i De - us,

2. *Et secundum multitudinem, mise* - ra - ti - onum tu -a - rum,
3. *Amplius lava me, ab i* - - - ni - qui - ta - te me - a,
4. *Quoniam, iniquitatem meam*...... e - go cog - nos - co,
5. *Tibi soli peccavi, et*............*malum coram te fe* - ci,
6. *Ecce enim in iniqui* - - - ta - ti - bus con - ceptus sum
7. *Ecce enim veri* - - - - ta - tem di - lex - is - ti,
8. *Asperges me hys* - - - so - po et mun - da - bor,
9. *Auditui meo dabis*............ *gaudium et lae* - ti - tiam
10. *Averte faciem tuam*......... . a pec-ca-tis me - is,
11. *Cor mundum*................. cre- a in me, De - us,
12. *Ne projicias*................ me a fa - cie tu - a,
13. *Redde mihi laetitiam*..........∙... sa - lu - ta - ris tu - i,
14. *Docebo*................... iniquos vi - as tu - as,
15. *Libera me de sanguinibus, Deus, Deus* sa - lu - tis me - ae,
16. *Domine,*................... la - bia mea a - pe-ri -es,
17. *Quoniam si voluisses sacrificium,*.. de - dis - sem u - ti - que
18. *Sacrificium Deo spiritus*......... con - tri-bu - la - tus,
19. *Benigne fac, Domine, in bona volun-* ta - te tu - a Si - on,
20. *Tunc acceptabis sacrificium justitiae,*
   oblationes, et hol -o caus - ta,
21. *Gloria*..................... Pa - tri et Fi - lio.
22. *Sicut erat in principio;*.......... et nunc et sem - per

* secundum magnam mi - - - - se - ri - cor - diam tu - am. 2

* dele i - - - - - -	ni - qui - ta - tem	me - am.	3.
* et a pec. - - - - - -	ca - to me - o	mundame.	4.
* et peccatum meum.....	con-tra me est	sem - per.	5.
* ut justificeris in sermonibus tuis, et	vincas cum judi - ca - ris.		6
* et in peccatis concepit.............	me ma - ter	me - a.	7.
* incerta et occulta sapientiae tuaé,......	manifes-tas - ti	mi - hi.	8.
* lavabis me, et super...............	ni - vem de - al - ba -	bor.	9
* et exultabunt ossa..................	hu - mi - li - a -	ta.	10
* et omnes iniqui - - - -	ta - tes me - as	de - le.	11.
* et Spiritum rectum innova...........	in vi - sceribus	me - is.	12
* et Spiritum sanctum tuum...........	ne au fer is	a me.	13
* et spiritu.....................	prin-ci - pali con - firma me.		14
* et impii...............	ad te con -ver - ten - tur.		15.
* et exultabit lingua..................	mea jus-ti - tiam	tu - am.	16.
* et os meum annunti - - -	a - bit lau - dem	tu - am.	17.
* holocaus - - - - -	tis non de - leo - ta - beris.		18.
* cor contritum et humilia'um,.........	De - us non des - pi - cies.		19.
* ut aedificentur....................	mu - - ri Je - rusa-lem.		20.
* tunc imponent super al - - -	ta - re tu - um	vi - tulos.	21.
* et......................	Spi - ri - tui	Sanc -to.	22
* et in saecula.................	sae - cu - lo - rum. A - men.		

"Desire of Heaven. Concluded.

joys have fad-ed and per-ished, Oh let me Thy splendors be-hold, Then let me taste thy joys un-told; Then let me taste thy joys un-told, Then let me taste thy joys un-told.

D.C.

THE YOKE OF CHRIST.

TWO or FOUR VOICES.   PLEYEL.

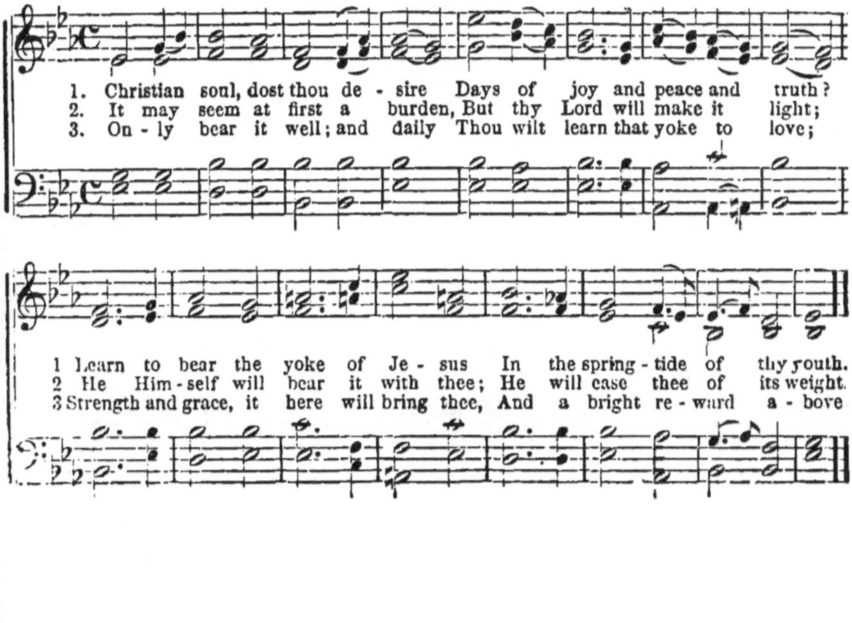

1. Christian soul, dost thou de-sire Days of joy and peace and truth?
2. It may seem at first a burden, But thy Lord will make it light;
3. On-ly bear it well; and daily Thou wilt learn that yoke to love;

1 Learn to bear the yoke of Je-sus In the spring-tide of thy youth.
2 He Him-self will bear it with thee; He will ease thee of its weight.
3 Strength and grace, it here will bring thee, And a bright re-ward a-bove

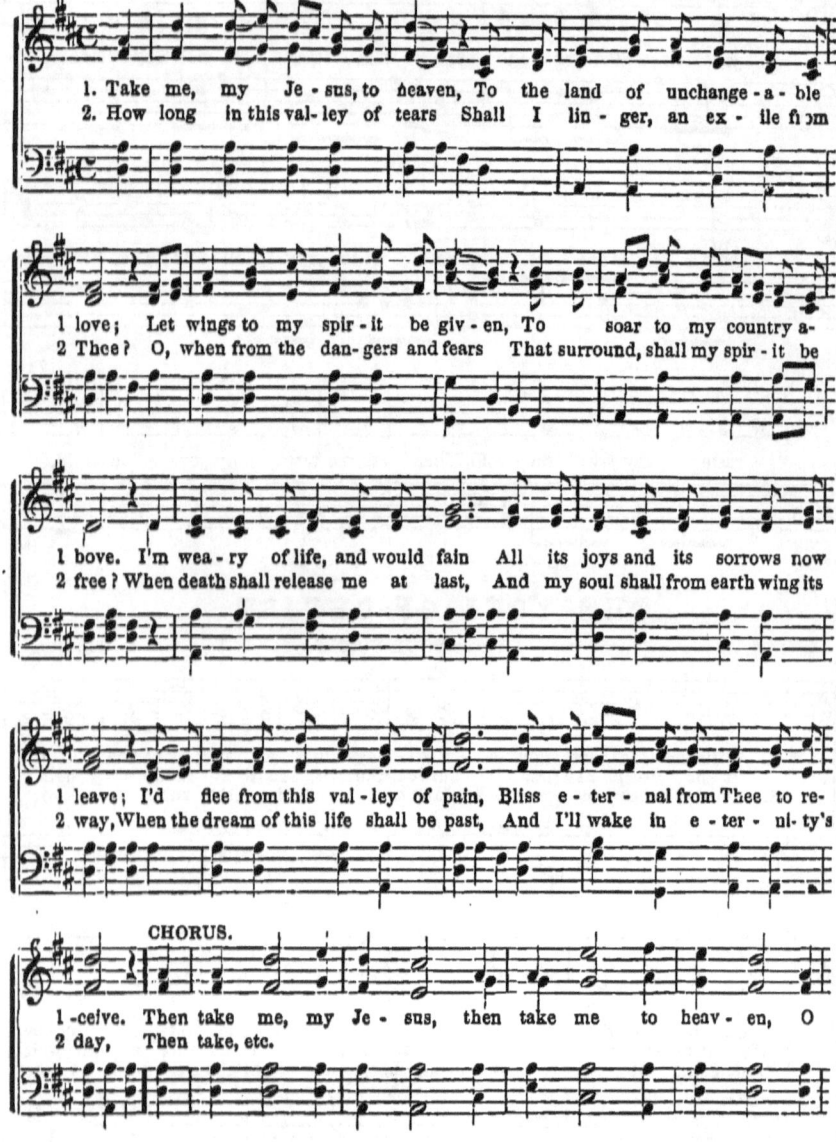

"Take Me, my Jesus." Concluded.

take me, my Je - sus, O take me to heav - en.

PRAY FOR THE DEAD.

QUARTET. W. DRESSLER.

1. Pray for the Dead! at noon and eve.... Lift up to
2. Pray for the Dead! tho' faith - ful they,... Yet while their
3. Pray for the Dead! thy pray'rs, tho' weak,.. May yet be
4. Pray for the Dead in ho - ly fear,... Pray that their

1 God thy fond re - quest; Im - plore his good - ness
2 pen - al - ties re - main, Must suff - 'ring purge the
3 heard and bring them ease; For God will hear thy
4 stains may be for - giv'n, That thou, thy - self, may

1 to re - lieve The suff - 'ring souls and grant them rest.
2 debt a - way, And pen - ance cleanse the sin - ful stain.
3 sighs, if meek,— Thy tears, if of - fered up for peace.
4 leave the bier, To en - ter pure at once in heav'n.

COMMON VESPERS OF THE SUNDAY.

The officiating Priest, having said the "*Pater Noster*" and "*Ave Maria*" in secret, will sing as follows:

Priest.

Deus in adju - - - to - rum meum in - ten - de.

Gloria Patri et Fi - lio et Spi - ri - tui Sanc - - to,

Slow.

Et in saecula saecu - lo - rum, A - - men. Al - le - lu - ia.

DIXIT DOMINUS. Psalm 109.

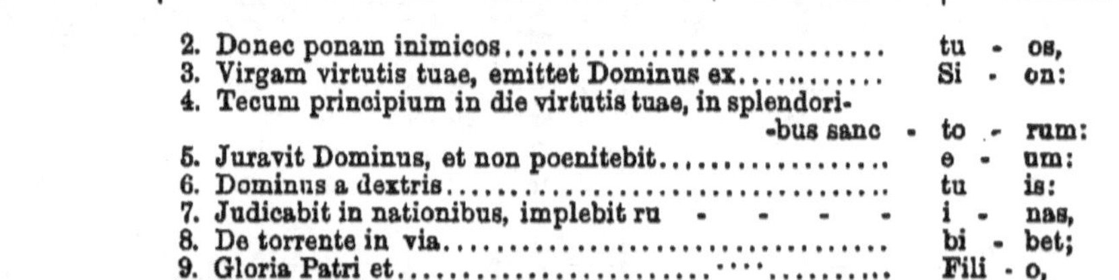

1. Dix - it Dominus, Domino.................... me - o,
2. Donec ponam inimicos..................... tu - os,
3. Virgam virtutis tuae, emittet Dominus ex........... Si - on:
4. Tecum principium in die virtutis tuae, in splendori-
   -bus sanc - to - rum:
5. Juravit Dominus, et non poenitebit................. e - um:
6. Dominus a dextris........................ tu - is:
7. Judicabit in nationibus, implebit ru - - - - i - nas,
8. De torrente in via....................... bi - bet;
9. Gloria Patri et.......................... Fili - o,
10. Sicut erat in principio, et nunc, et................ sem - per

CONFITEBOR. Psalm 110.

1. Con-fi-tebor tibi, Domine, in toto.................... cor - de   me - o,
2. Magna... ope - ra   Domi-ni ;
3. Confessio et magnificentia.. .... o - pus   e - jus :
4. Memoriam fecit mirabilium suorum, misericors
   et mise - ra - tor   Domi-nus:
5. Memor erit in saeculum testa - - - men - ti   su- i :
6. Ut det illis haeredi - - - - - ta - tem   gen-tium :
7. Fidelia omnia mandata ejus, confirmata in..... saecu-lum   saecu-li.
8. Redemptionem misit......................... popu-lo   su - o,
9. Sanctum terribile............................ no - men   e - jus :
10. Intellectus bonus omnibus faci - - - enti- bus   e - um :
11. Gloria.. Pa - tri, et Fi - lio,
12. Sicut erat in principio, et.................... nunc, et   sem - per,

BEATUS VIR. Psalm 111.

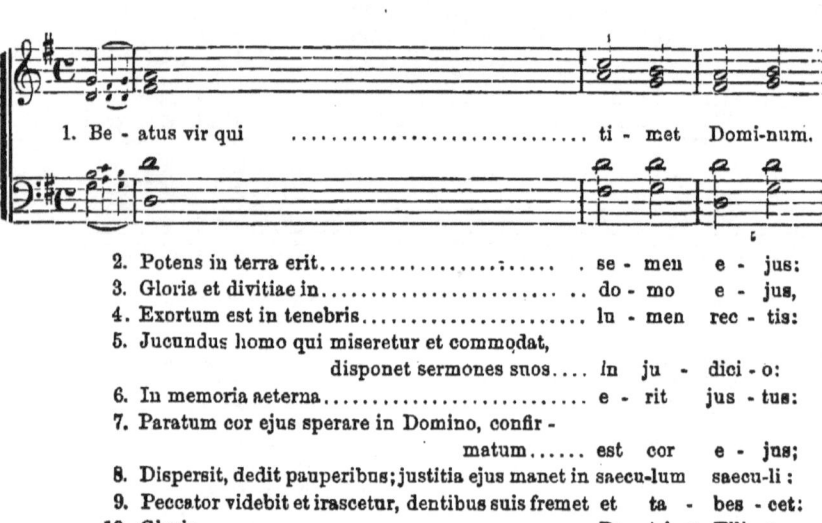

1. Be - atus vir qui .... ti - met   Domi-num.
2. Potens in terra erit........................ . se - men   e - jus:
3. Gloria et divitiae in...................... .. do - mo   e - jus,
4. Exortum est in tenebris.................... lu - men   rec - tis:
5. Jucundus homo qui miseretur et commodat,
   disponet sermones snos.... In ju - dici - o:
6. In memoria aeterna........................ e - rit   jus - tus:
7. Paratum cor ejus sperare in Domino, confir -
   matum...... est cor   e - jus;
8. Dispersit, dedit pauperibus; justitia ejus manet in saecu-lum   saecu-li :
9. Peccator videbit et irascetur, dentibus suis fremet et   ta - bes - cet:
10. Gloria.. Pa - tri, et Fili - o,
11. Sicut erat in principio, et.................... nunc, et   sem - per.

* in consilio justorum, et congre - - - ga - ti - o - ne. 2.

* exquisita in omnes volun - - - - ta - tes e - jus. 3
* et justitia ejus manet in. . . . . saecu - lum sae - cu - li. 4

* escam. . . . . dedit ti - men-tibus se. 5.
* virtutem operum suorum annuntiabit. . . . . po - pulo su - o ; 6.
* opera manuum ejus veritas. . . . . et ju - di - cium. 7.
* facta in veritate et. . . . . ae - qui - ta - te. 8.
* mandavit in aeternum testa - - - men - tum su - um. 9.
* initium sapientiae. . . . . ti - mor Do - mi - ni. 10.
* laudatio ejus manet in. saecu - lum sae - cu - li. 11.
* et Spi - - - - - - - - - - - ri - tui Sanc - to. 12.
* et in saecula saecu - - - - - - lo - rum. A - - men.

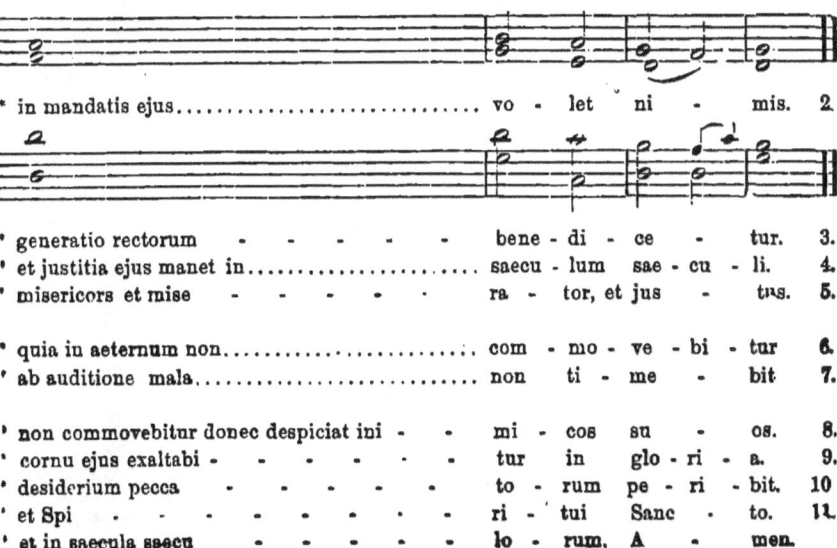

* in mandatis ejus. . . . . vo - let ni - mis. 2.

* generatio rectorum - - - - - - bene - di - ce - tur. 3.
* et justitia ejus manet in. . . . . saecu - lum sae - cu - li. 4.
* misericors et mise - - - - - - ra - tor, et jus - tus. 5.

* quia in aeternum non. . . . . com - mo - ve - bi - tur 6.
* ab auditione mala. . . . . non ti - me - bit 7.

* non commovebitur donec despiciat ini - - mi - cos su - os. 8.
* cornu ejus exaltabi - - - - - - tur in glo - ri - a. 9.
* desiderium pecca - - - - - - to - rum pe - ri - bit. 10
* et Spi - - - - - - - - - ri - tui Sanc - to. 11.
* et in saecula saecu - - - - - - lo - rum, A - men.

LAUDATE PUERI. Psalm 112.

1. Lau - date.. pueri .... Domi - num,
2. Sit nomen Domini bene - - - - dic - tum,
3. A solis ortu usque ad oc - - - - ca - sum,
4. Excelsus super omnes gentes.............. Domi - nus,
5. Quis sicut Dominus Deus noster, qui in altis.... habi - tat,
6. Suscitans a terra........................ ino - pem,
7. Ut collocet eum, cum prin - - - - cipi - bus,
8. Qui habitare facit sterilem in............ do - mo,
9. GloriaPatri et........................... Fi - lio,
10. Sicut erat in principio, et nunc, et········........ sem - per,

IN EXITU IN ISRAEL. Psalm 113.
(TO BE SUNG WHEN THERE IS NO FEAST.)

1. In.... exitu Israel.................... de Æ - gyp - to.
2. Facta est Judæa sanctifi - - - - ca - tio e - jus,
3. Mare................................... vi - dit, et fu - git,
4. Montes exultaverunt.................... ut a - rie - tes,
5. Quid est tibi, mare,................... quod fu - gis - ti?
6. Montes exultastis...................... si - cut a - rie - tes,
7. A facie Domini........................ mo - ta est ter - ra,
8. Qui convertit petram in................ stag - na a - qua - rum,
9. Non nobis,............................. Domi - ne non no - bis,
10. Super misericordia tua et veri - - - ta - te tu - a:
11. Deus autem............................ nos - ter in coe - lo;
12. Simulacra gentium ar - - - - - gen - tum et an - rum,
13. Os habent, et....... .... non lo - quen-tur,
14. Aures habent,......................... et non au - dient,
15. Manus habent, et non palpabunt; pedes
    habent, et non.... am - bu - la - bunt;
16. Similes illis fiant qui................ fa - ciunt e - a:
17. Domus Israel spe - - - - - - ra - vit in Do - mino:
18. Domus Aaron spe - - - - - - ra - vit in Do - mino:
19. Qui timent Dominum, spera - - -, ve - runt in Do - mino:
20. Dominus memor........................ fu - it nos - tri,
21. Benedixit............................. Do - mui Is - rael,
22. Benedixit omnibus qui................. ti - ment Do - minum,
23 Adjiciat.............................. Do - minus su - per vos,
24. Benedicti............................ vos a Do - mino:
25. Coelum............................... coe - li Do - mino:
26. Non mortui lau - - - - - - dabunt te, Do - mine,
27. Sed nos qui vivimus, bene - - - dici - mus Do - mino
28. Gloria............................... Pa - tri, et Fi - lio,
29. Sicut erat in principio, et.......... nunc, et sem - per,

* laudate............................ no - men   Do - mi - ni.   2.

* ex hoc nunc, et us - - - - -   que   in   sae - cu - lum.   3.
* laudibile........................   no - men   Do mi - ni.   4.
* et super coelos glo - - - -   ri - a   e - jus.   5.
* et humilia respicit in coelo........ et   in   ter - ra?   3.
* et de stercore................... eri - gens   pau-pe - rem.   7.
* cum principibus - - - - -   po - puli   su - i.   8.
* matrem fili - - - - - -   orum   lae -   tan - tem.   9.
* et Spi - - - - - - -   ri - tui   Sanc - to.   10.
* et in saecula saecu - - - -   lo - rum.   A - men.

* domus Jacob de.................... po - pulo   bar - ba - ro.   2.

* Israel po - - - - - -   tes - tas   e - - jus.   3.
* Jordanis conversus................ est   re - tror - sum.   4.
* et colles, sicut.................. ag - ni   o - vi - um.   5.
* et tu Jordanis, quia conversus.... es   re - tror - sum?   6.
* et colles, sicut.................. ag - ni   o - vi - um?   7.
* a facie.......................... De - i   Ja - cob.   8.
* et rupem in...................... fon - tes a - qua - rum.   9.
* sed nomini....................... tuo   da   glo - ri - am.   10.
* nequando dicant gentes: Ubi est.... Deus   e - o   rum?   11.
* omnia quaecumque................. vo - luit.   fe - cit.   12.
* opera............................ ma - nuum   ho - mi - num.   13.
* occulos habent, et............... non   vi - de - bunt.   14.
* nares habent, et non............. o   - do - ra - bunt.   15.
* non clamabunt in................. gut - ture   su - o.   16.
* et omnes qui con - - - - -   fidunt in   e - - is.   17.
* adjutor eorum, et pro - - - -   tector e - o - rum est.   18.
* adjutor eorum, et pro - - - -   tector e - o - rum est.   19.
* adjutor eorum, et pro - - - -   tector e - o - rum est.   20.
* et bene - - - - - - -   dix - it   no - bis.   21.
* benedixit'....................... do - mui   Aa - ron.   22.
* pusillis......................... cum   ma - jo - ri - bus.   23.
* super vos, et super.............. fi - lios   ves - tros.   24.
* qui fecit........................ coelum et   ter - ram.   25.
* terram autem dedit............... fi - liis   ho - mi - num   26.
* neque omnes que descendunt........ in   in   fer - num.   27.
* ex hoc nunc et................... usque in   sae - cu - lum. 28.
* et Spi - - - - - - -   ri - tui   Sanc - to.   29.
* et in saecula saecu - - - -   lo - rum.   A - - men.

LAUDATE DOMINUM. No. 1. Psalm 116

To be sung on Sundays when there is a Feast instead of "*In Exitu Israel*," also sung after the Benediction.

1. Laudate Dominum omnes gentes, laudate eum omnes populi.
2. Quoniam confirmata est super nos miseri-cordia e-jus et veritas Domini manet in ae-ter-num.
3. Gloria Pa-tri et Fi-li-o et Spi - - - ri-tui Sanc-to.
4. Sicut erat in principio, et nunc et sem-per et in saecula saeculo-rum, A-men.

LAUDATE DOMINUM. No. 2.

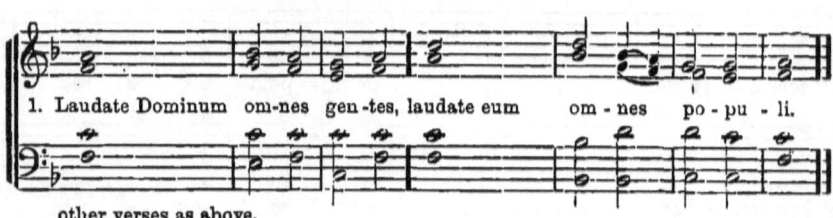

1. Laudate Dominum omnes gen-tes, laudate eum om-nes po-pu-li.

other verses as above.

LAUDATE DOMINUM. No. 3.

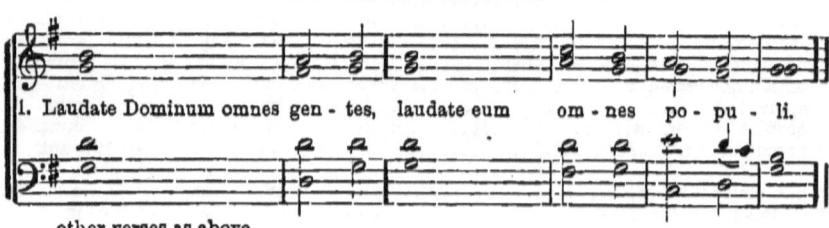

1. Laudate Dominum omnes gen-tes, laudate eum om-nes po-pu-li.

other verses as above

After the Priest has read the "*Capitulum*," or little chapter, the Choir responds as follows:

Deo gra-ti-as.

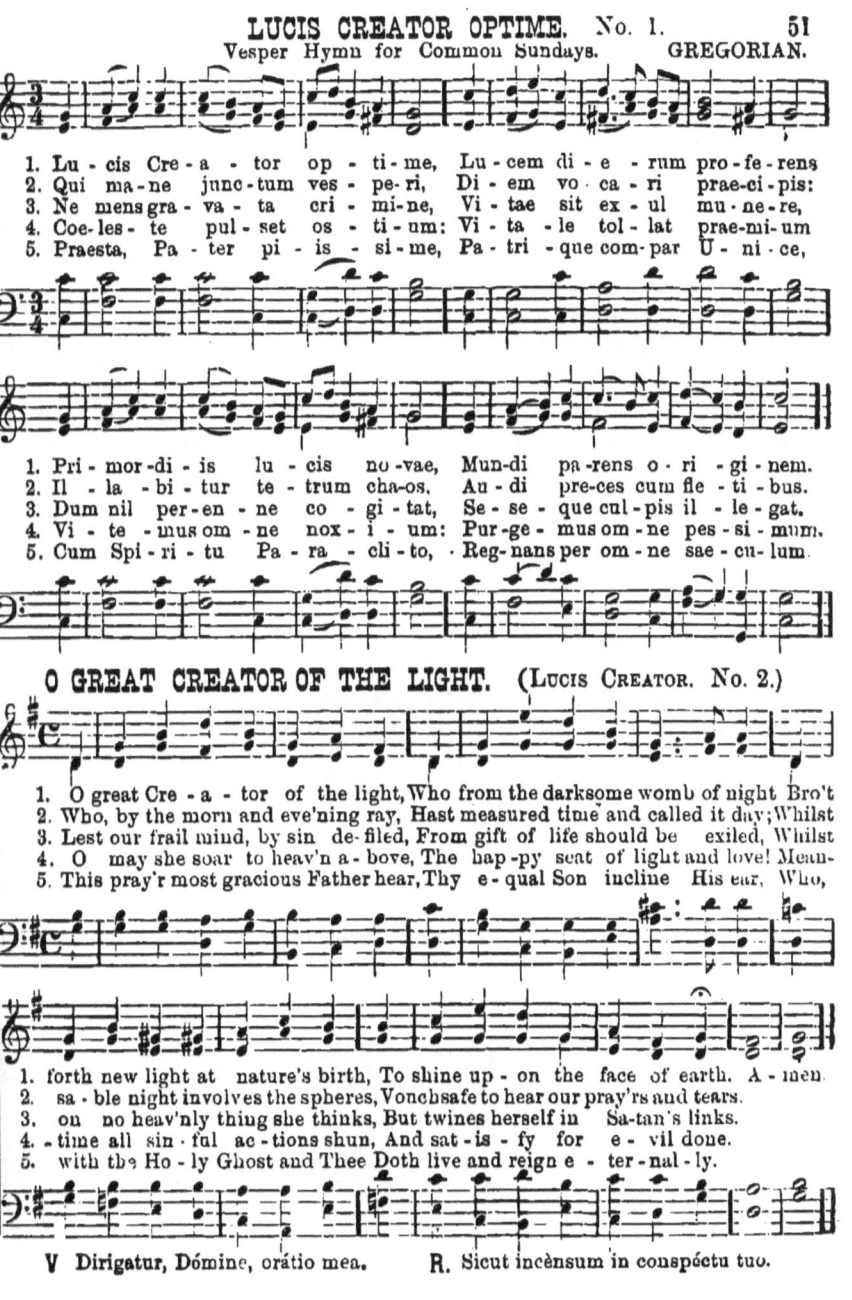

MAGNIFICAT. Canticle of the Blessed Virgin. St. Luke, I

1. Mag — nifi - cat
2. Et ex - ul - tavit spiritus .... me - us
3. Qui - a res - pexit humilitatem ancillae .... su - ae;
4. Qui - a fecit mihi magna, qui .... potens est,
5. Et mi - sericordia ejus a progenie in pro — — ge - nies
6. Fe - cit po - tentiam in brachio .... su - o,
7. De - po-su - it potentes de .... se - de,
8. E - su -ri - entes implevit .... bo - nis,
9. Sus - ce-pit Israel puerum .... su - um,
10. Si - cut lo - cutus est ad patres .... nos - tros,
11. Glo - - ria Patri, et .... Fili - o,
12. Si - cut erat in principio et nunc, et .... sem -per,

RESPONSES AFTER MAGNIFICAT.

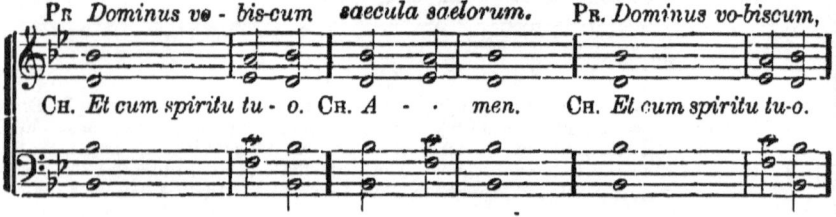

Pr. Oremus, &c.
Pr. Dominus vo - bis-cum   saecula saelorum.   Pr. Dominus vo-biscum,
Ch. Et cum spiritu tu - o. Ch. A - - men.   Ch. Et cum spiritu tu-o.

The manner of singing the *Benedicamus Domino* and Response, varies according to the feast and season, and at the option of the Priest. The choir should listen attentively and respond with the *Deo Gratias* in the same tone and manner.

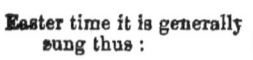

Easter time it is generally sung thus:

Pr. Benedicamus Do - mi - no
Ch. Deo .... gra - ti - as

Then follows one of the Antiphons of the Blessed Virgin according to the season.

ALMA REDEMPTORIS.

Antiphon of the B. V. M. from 1st Sunday in Advent to Purification.

TWO-PART CHORUS. — GORIA.

1. Al-ma Re-dempto- ris Ma - ter, quæ per-vi- a cœ - li, Por-ta ma - nes, et stel - la ma - ris suc - cur - re, ca - den - ti. Sur - ge - re qui curat po - pu - lo: Tu quæ ge-nu-is - ti, natu - ra mi - ran - te, tu - um sanc - tum, Ge-ni- to - rem.
2. Vir-go, pri - us. ac pos-te - ri - us, Gabrie-lis ab o - re, Su - mens, il - lud, A - ve pec-ca- -torum, mi - se - re - re.

FINE.

D.S.

IN ADVENT. **V**. *Angelus Dómini nuntiávit Mariæ.* **R**. *Et concépit de Spi-*
[*ritu Sancto*
AFTER ADVENT. **V**. *Post partum Virgo inviolata pérmansisti.* **R**. *Dei géni-*
trix intercede pro nobis. **Pr**. *Oremus, etc.* **Ch**. *Amen.*
Then follows the Benediction of the Blessed Sacrament. "Tantum Ergo"

AVE REGINA

Antiphon of the B. V. M. from Purification till Easter.

SOLO & THREE-PART CHORUS with BASS ad lib.   WEBBE.

1. A - ve Re - gi - na, Re-gi - na cœ- lo - rum, A - ve Do-mi-na, an - ge - lo - rum: Sal - ve ra - dix, sal - ve por - ta, Ex qua mun - do Lux est or - ta, Ex qua mun - do, Lux est or - ta.
2. Gau - de Vir - go, glo - ri - o - sa Su - per om - nes, spe - ci - o - sa. Va - le, va - le, O val - de de - co - ra, Et pro no - bis Chris- tum ex - o - ra, Et pro no - bis, Chris- tum ex - o - ra.

℣. *Dignare me, laudare te, Virgo sacrata.*   ℟. *Da mihi virtutem contra hostes tuos.*

Pr. *Oremus, etc.*   Ch. *Amen.*

Then follows the Benediction of the B. S. "Tantum Ergo."

SALVE REGINA.

Antiphon of the B. V. M. from Trinity till Advent.
DUET or TWO-PART CHORUS. — STERR.

1. Sal - ve, Re - gi - na, Ma - ter mi - se - ri - cor - diæ, 2
2. Vi - ta dul - ce - do, et spes nos - tra, sal - ve. 3
3. Ad te cla - ma - mus, ex - u - les fi - lii E - vae, Ad et sus-pi-
4. Ei - a er - go ad - vo - ca - ta, nos - tra, il - los tu - os
3. -ra - mus, ge - men - tes et flen - tes, in hoc la-cry-ma-rum val - le 4
4. -mi - se - ri - cor - des o - cu - los ad nos con - ver - te 5
5. Et Je - sum be - ne - dic - tum fruc - tum ven - tris tu - i, 6
6. no - bis post hoc ex - i - li - um os - ten - de. 7
7. O Cle - mens! O Pi - a! O dul - cis Vir - go Ma - ri - a!

V. Ora pro nobis, sancta Dei *genetrix* R. Ut digni efficiamur promissionibus Christi. Pr. Oremus, etc. Ch. Amen.
Then follows the Benediction of the Blessed Sacrament. "Tantum Ergo."

VESPERS FOR THE FEASTS OF THE BLESSED VIRGIN MARY.

Domine ad adjuvandum, p. 44, Dixit Dominus, p. 44, Laudate Pueri, p. 48, and the following.

LAETATUS SUM. Psalm 121.

1. Laetatus sum in his quae............................ dicta sunt mi - hi:
2. Stantes erant.. pe - des nos - tri:
3. Jerusalem, quae aedifi - - - - - - catur ut civi - tas,
4. Illuc enim ascenderunt tribus...................... tri - bus Domi-ni,
5. Quia illic sederunt sedes .... in ju - di - cio,
6. Rogate quae ad pacem............................... sunt Je - rusa - lem :
7. Fiat pax in vir - - - - - - - tu - te tu - a,
8. Propter fratres meos et prox - - - - - - i - mos me - os,
9. Propter domum Domini............................... De - i nos - tri,
Gloria... Patri, et Fi - lio,
Sicut erat in principio, et......................... nunc, et sem - per,

NISI DOMINUS. Psalm 126.

1. Nisi Dominus aedifi - - - - - - - - cave-rit Do - mum,
2. Nisi Dominus custodierit .... ci - vi - ta - tem,
3. Vanum est vobis ante............................. lu - cem surge-re ;
4. Cum dederit dilectis............................. su - is somnum ;
5. Sicut sagittae in ma - - - - - - - - nu - po - ten - tis,
6. Beatus vir qui implevit desiderium su - - - - um ex ip - sis :
Gloria.. Patri et Fi - lio,
Sicut erat in principio, et...................... nunc, et sem - per,

LAUDA JERUSALEM. Psalm 147.

1. Lau - - da Jerusalem... Dominum:
2. Quoniam confortavit seras portarum tu - - - a - rum ;
3. Qui posuit fines tuos;... pa - cem,
4. Qui emittit eloquium suum .... ter - rae ;
5. Qui dat nivem sicut .... la - nam ;
6. Mittet crystallum suum, sicut buc - - - - cel - las ;
7. Emittit verbum suum, et liquefaciet................... e - a :
8. Qui annuntiat verbum suum .... Ja - cob,
9. Non fecit taliter omni nati - - - - - - o - ni,
Gloria Patri, et.. Fi - lio,
Sicut erat in principio, et nunc, et......... .... sem - per,

PRIEST READS *CAPITULUM,* **OR LITTLE CHAPTER. CHOIR RESPOND:** *DEO GRATIAS.* **THEN**

ALSO OF VIRGINS AND HOLY WOMEN.

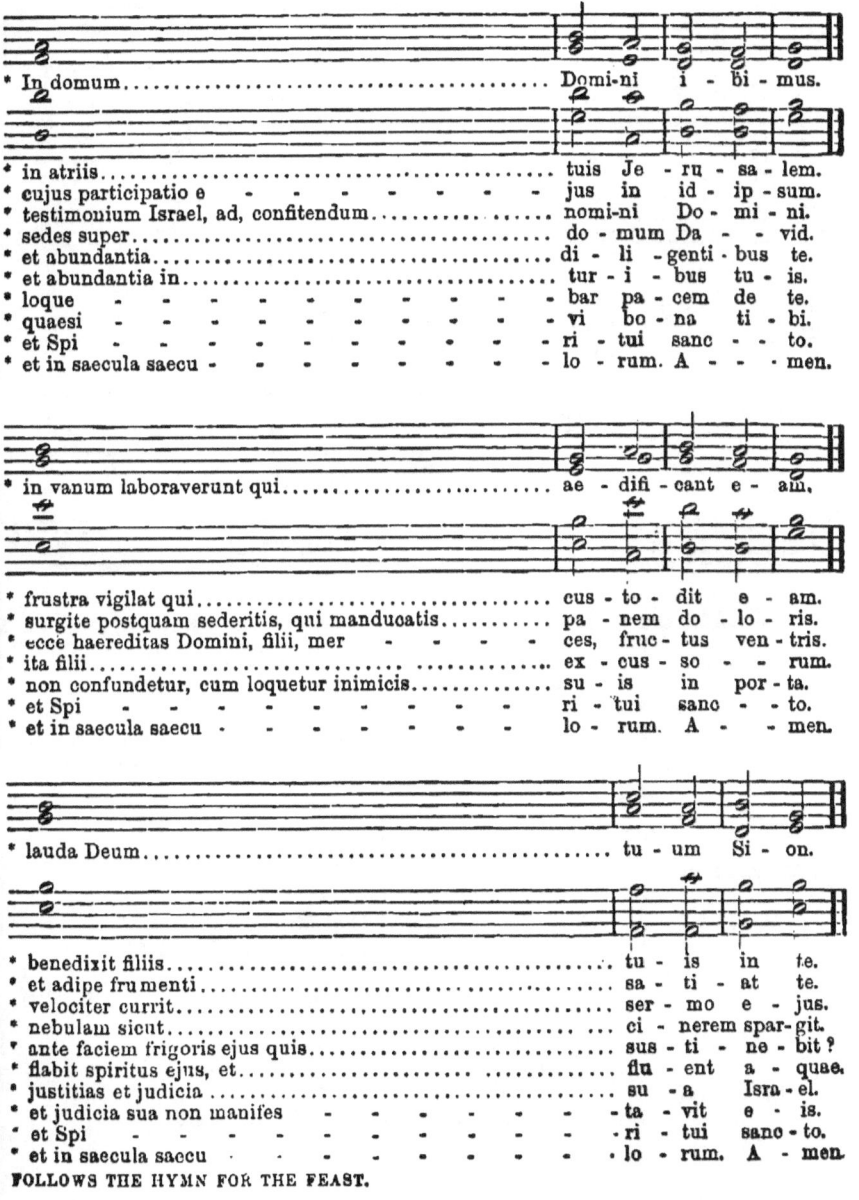

* In domum... Do-mi-ni i - bi - mus.

* in atriis.. tuis Je - ru - sa - lem.
* cujus participatio e - - - - - - - - jus in id - ip - sum.
* testimonium Israel, ad, confitendum............... nomi-ni Do - mi - ni.
* sedes super... do - mum Da - - vid.
* et abundantia.. di - li - genti - bus te.
* et abundantia in.................................... tur - i - bus tu - is.
* loque - - - - - - - - - bar pa - cem de te.
* quaesi - - - - - - - - - vi bo - na ti - bi.
* et Spi - - - - - - - - - ri - tui sanc - - to.
* et in saecula saecu - - - - - - - - lo - rum. A - - - men.

* in vanum laboraverunt qui......................... ae - difi - cant e - am,

* frustra vigilat qui.................................. cus - to - dit e - am.
* surgite postquam sederitis, qui manducatis.......... pa - nem do - lo - ris.
* ecce haereditas Domini, filii, mer - - - - ces, fruc - tus ven - tris.
* ita filii... ex - cus - so - - rum.
* non confundetur, cum loquetur inimicis............ su - is in por - ta.
* et Spi - - - - - - - - ri - tui sanc - - to.
* et in saecula saecu - - - - - - - lo - rum. A - - men.

* lauda Deum.. tu - um Si - on.

* benedixit filiis....................................... tu - is in te.
* et adipe frumenti................................... sa - ti - at te.
* velociter currit..................................... ser - mo e - jus.
* nebulam sicut....................................... ci - nerem spar-git.
* ante faciem frigoris ejus quis..................... sus - ti - ne - bit ?
* flabit spiritus ejus, et............................. flu - ent a - quae.
* justitias et judicia................................. su - a Isra - el.
* et judicia sua non manifes - - - - - - ta - vit e - is.
* et Spi - - - - - - - - ri - tui sanc - to.
* et in saecula saecu - - - - - - - lo - rum. A - men.

FOLLOWS THE HYMN FOR THE FEAST.

AVE MARIS STELLA. No. 1.

Versicles and Responses, for the various Feasts of the Blessed Virgin.

CONCEPTION. **V** *Conceptio est hodie sanctæ Mariæ Virginis.*
            R *Cujus vita inclyta cunctas illustrat Ecclesias.*
PURIFICATION. **V** *Responsum accepit Simeon a Spiritu Sancto.*
            R *Non visurum se mortem, nisi vederet Christum Domini.*
ANNUNCIATION. **V** *Ave Maria plena.* (In Paschal Time add.) *Alleluja.*
            R *Dominus tecum.*
VISITATION. **V** *Benedicta tu in mulieribus.*
            R *Et benedictus fructus ventris tui.*
ASSUMPTION. **V** *Exaltata est sancta Dei genetrix.*
            R *Super chorus angelorum ad cœlestia regna.*
NATIVITY. **V** *Nativitas est hodie sanctæ Mariæ Virginis.*
            R *Cujus vita inclyta cunctas illustrat Ecclesias.*

All other Festivals of the Blessed Virgin Mary.

1st VESPERS. **V** *Dignare me, laudare te, Virgo sacrata.*
            R *Da mihi virtutem contra hostes tuos.*
2d VESPERS. **V** *Diffusa est gratia in labiis tuis.*
            R *Propterea benedixit te Deus in æternum.*

AVE MARIS STELLA. No. 2.

DUET or TWO-PART CHORUS.   Arr. from BLUMENTHAL.

DUET and TWO-PART CHORUS.

Music by LAMBILLOTTE.

1. Come, O Divine Messiah! Oh! haste, we're weary waiting thee; On earth we nought desire, Save Thee, sweet One in Three. Oh, quick descend, bid time take wing! Else our poor hearts no peace will know, But fiercer with impatience glow.

2. Wilt leave Thy Father's home For us who languish here with love, And 'neath our fetters groan! Awaiting aid from above. Oh! come! Oh! come! bid time take wing! We'll deck our hearts with brilliants rare, And welcome meet for Thee prepare.

3. Think not upon our baseness; Take vengeance not upon our crimes, But with us yet have patience, Make us all thine in time. For art not Thou our Lord and God? To whom should we for refuge flee, If not, O Lord our God, to Thee.

"Hymn for Advent." Concluded.

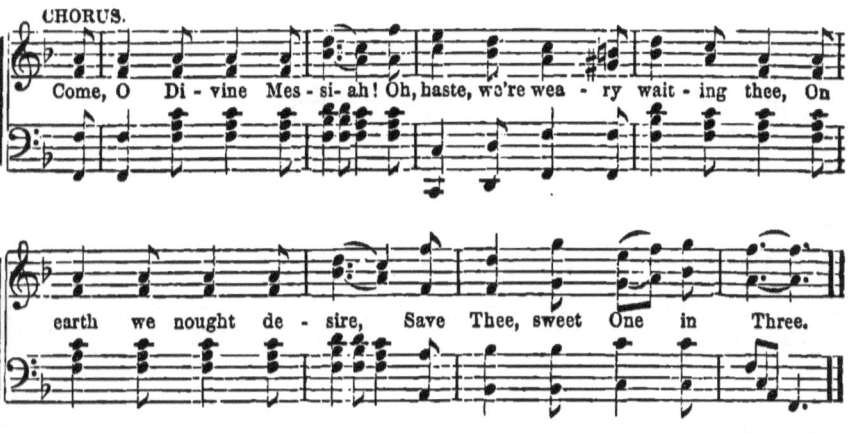

CREATOR ALME SIDERUM.

Vesper Hymn for the Sundays in Advent.

DUET or TWO-PART CHORUS, or QUARTET.   GREGORIAN.

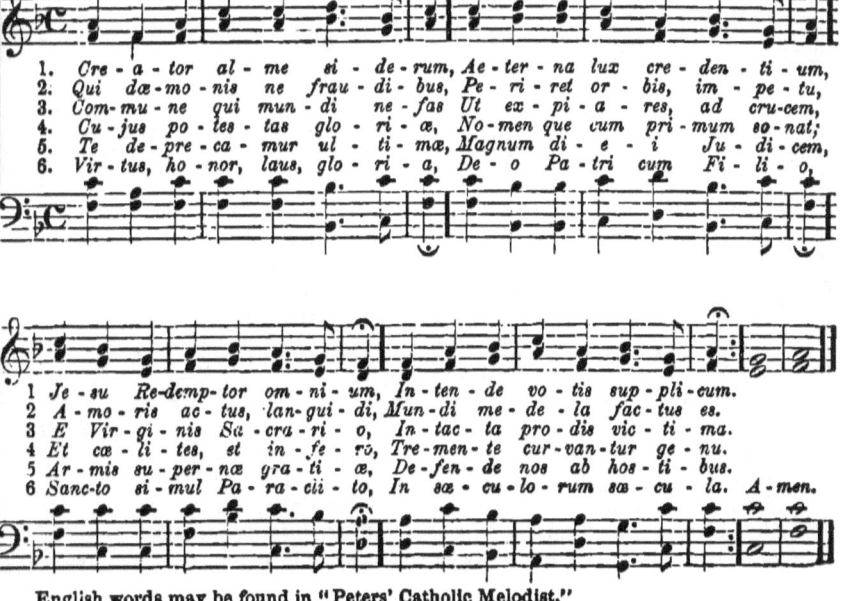

English words may be found in "Peters' Catholic Melodist."

JESU REDEMPTOR OMNIUM.
VESPER HYMN FOR CHRISTMAS DAY.
FOR 2 OR 4 VOICES.　　　WESTLAKE.

1. Je-su Redemp-tor om-ni-um, Quem lu-cis ante o-ri-gi-nem Pa-rem Pa-ter-nae glo-ri-ae Pa-ter su-pre-mus e-di-dit.
2. Tu, lu-men et splen-dor Pa-tris, Tu, spes per-en-nis om-ni-um, In-ten-de, quas fun--dunt pre-ces Tu-i per or-bem ser-vu-li.
3. Me-men-to, re-rum Con-di-tor, No-stri quod o-lim cor-po-ris, Sa-cra-ta ab al-vo Vir-gi-nis Na-scen-do, for-mam sump-se-ris.
4. Tes-ta-tur hoc prae-sens di-es, Cur-rens per an-ni cir-cu-lum, Quod so-lus e si-nu Pa-tris Mundi sa-lus ad-ve-ne-ris.
5. Hunc as-tra, tel-lus, ae-quo-ra, Hunc om-ne, quod coe-lo sub-est, Sa-lu-tis auc-to--rem no-vae No-vo sa-lu-tat can-ti-co.

6.
Et nos, beata quos sacri
Rigavit unda sanguinis,
Natalis ob diem tui
Hymni tributum solvimus,

7.
Jesu, tibi sit gloria,
Qui natus es de Virgine,
Cum Patre, et almo Spiritu,
In sempiterna saecula,

A-men.

N. B. The English words of this Hymn will be found in PETERS' CATHOLIC MELODIST.

O SALUTARIS.

TWO VOICES & BASS AD LIB.

TANTUM ERGO. No. 1.

THREE-PART CHORUS.

1. Tan - tum er - go Sa - cra - men - tum, Ve - ne - re - mur
2. Ge - ni - to - ri, ge - ni - to - que Laus et ju - bi-

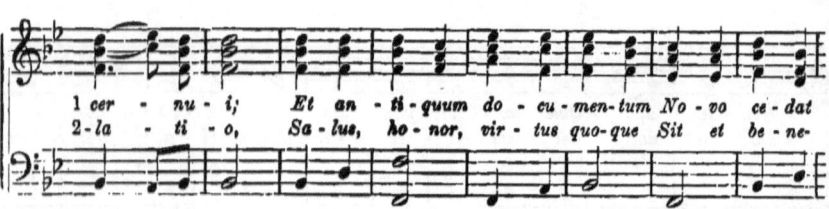

1 cer - nu - i; Et an - ti - quum do - cu - men - tum No - vo ce - dat
2 - la - ti - o, Sa - lus, ho - nor, vir - tus quo - que Sit et be - ne -

1 ri - tu - i; Præ - stet fi - des sup - ple - men - tum Sen - su - um
2 - dic - ti - o; Pro - ce - den - ti ab u - tro - que Com - par sit

1 sen - su - um sen - su - um de - fec - tu - i. A - men.
2 com - par sit com - par sit lau - da - ti - o. A - men.

Pr. *Panem de cœli, etc.* **R** *Omne delectamentum in se habentum.*

During Easter tide Alleluia is added.

TE DEUM.

SUNG AT BENEDICTION ON OCCASIONS OF THANKSGIVING.

GREGORIAN.

1. Te Deum lau - - - da - mus, te Dominum.... con - fi - te - mur.
2. Te aeternum............ Pa - trem omnis terra..... ve - ne - ra - tur.
3. Tibi omnes............ ange - li, tibi coeli, et uni-
versae.... po - tes - ta - tes:
4. Tibi cherubim et........ sera - phim, incessabili...... voce pro-cla-mant
5. Sanctus, sanctus........ sanc - tus, Dominus....... De - us Saba-oth:
6. Pleni sunt coeli et..... ter - ra. Majestatis...... glo - riae tu - ae.
7. Te glori - - - o - sus Aposto - lo - rum cho-rus.
8. Te Prophe - - - ta - rum; lau - - dabi - lis numerus.
9. Te Martyrum, candi - da - tus lau - - dat ex - erci-tus.
10. Te per orbem ter - ra - rum; sancta confi - tetur Ec - cle-sia.
11. Pa - - - - - trem, immensae...... ma - jes - ta - tis.
12. Venerandum tuum....... vo - rum, et............. uni - cum Fili-um.
13. Sanctum................ quo - que, Pa - - racli- tum Spiritum.
14. Tu Rex............... glo - riae, Chris - - - - te.
15. Tu.................. Pa - tris, sempi - - ternus es Fili-us.
16. Tu ad liberandum suscep-
- turus.... homi-nem, non horruisti... Virgi- nis ute-rum.
17. Tu devicto mortis a - cu - leo, aperuisti credenti-
bus..... regna coe-lo - rum
18. Tu ad dexteram Dei..... se - des, in............. glo - ria Pa- tris.
19. Judex...... crede-ris, es - - se ven- tu - rus.
(Kneel)20. Te ergo quaesumus, tuis
famulis.... subve-ni, quos pretioso san-
- guine.. re - de - mis-ti.
21. Aeterna fac cum Sanctis.. tu - is. in gloria....... nu - me - ra - ri.
22. Salvum fac populum tuum, Domi-ne, et benedic haciedi-ta - ti tu- ae.
23. Et rege eos, et extolle.... il - los usque.......... in ae - ter-num.
24. Per singulos........... di - es, bene - - dici-mus te.
25. Et laudamus nomen tuum in saecu-lum; et in............ saecu-lum saecu-li
26. Dignare, Domine, die.... is - to, sine peccato nos cus - to - di - re
27. Miserere nostri........ Domi-ne, mise - - re - re nos-tri.
28. Fiat misericordia tua, Do-
mine,...... super nos: quemadmodum spe-ravi-mus in te
29. In te, Domine, spe - ra - vi: non confundar... in ae - ter-num.

LITANY OF THE B. V. M.

Slow.

Ky - ri - e e - lei - son Ky - ri - e e - lei - son
Ky - ri - e e - lei - son Ky - ri - e e - lei - son
Pa - ter de coe - lis De - us Mi - se - re - re no - bis
Spi - ritus Sanc - te De - us Mi - se - re - re no - bis

Cheerfully.

Sanc - ta Ma - ri - a, Sanc - ta De - i Gen - i - trix,

* Ma - ter Chris - ti, Mater di - vi - nae gra - ti - ae,
Ma - ter cas - tis - si - ma, Mater in - vi - o - la - ta,
* Ma - ter a - ma - bi - lis, Ma - ter ad - mi - ra - bi - lis,
Mater sal - va - to - ris, Vir - go pru - den - tis - si - ma,
* *Virgo prae - di - can - da,* Vir - go po - tens,
Vir - go fi - de - lis, Spe - cu - lum jus - ti - ti - ae,
* *Causa nostrae lae - ti - ti - ae,* Vas spi - ri - tu - a - le,
Vas insigne de - vo - ti - o - nis, Ro - sa mys - ti - ca.
* Tur - ris e - bur - ne - a, Do - mus au - re - a,
Ja - nu - a coe - li, Stel - la ma - tu - ti - na,
* *Refugium pec - ca - to - rum,* *Consolatrix af - flic - to - rum,*
Regina an - ge - lo - rum, Regi - na patriar - cha - rum,
* *Regina a - pos - to - lo - rum,* Re - gi - na mar - ty - rum,
Re - gi - na vir - gi - num, O - ra pro - no - bis,
* *Regina sine labe originali) con - cep - ta,* O - ra pro - no - bis,

1. Agnus Dei qui tollis peccata mun - di, **Par - ce no - bis Do - mine.*
2. Agnus Dei qui tollis peccata mun - di, **Ex - au - di nos Do - mi - ne.*

V. *Ora pro nobis, sancta Dei Genitrix*

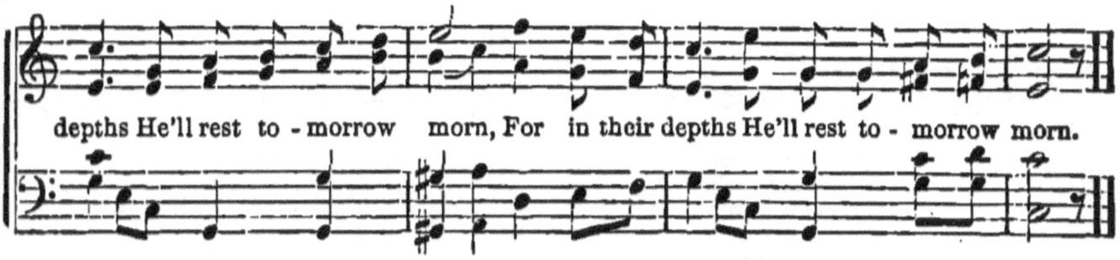

"Eve of Communion." Concluded.

depths He'll rest to-morrow morn, For in their depths He'll rest to-morrow morn.

(a.) IN THIS SACRAMENT, SWEET JESUS.
(b.) COME, SWEET JESUS.

CHORUS for TWO or FOUR VOICES.   MOZART.

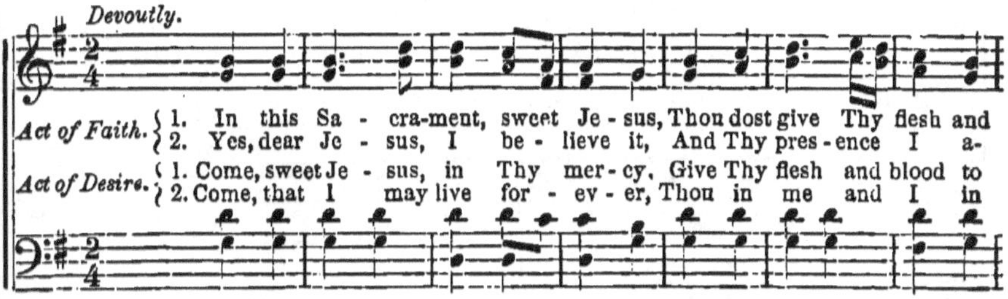

Devoutly.

Act of Faith. { 1. In this Sa - cra-ment, sweet Je-sus, Thou dost give Thy flesh and
           { 2. Yes, dear Je - sus, I be - lieve it, And Thy pres - ence I a-

Act of Desire. { 1. Come, sweet Je - sus, in Thy mer - cy, Give Thy flesh and blood to
           { 2. Come, that I may live for - ev - er, Thou in me and I in

a. { 1 blood, With Thy soul and God - head al - so, As our own most pre-cious food.
   { 2 -dore, And with all my heart I love Thee, May I love Thee more and more.

b. { 1 me; Come to me, O dear - est Je - sus, Come, my soul's true life to be.
   { 2 Thee; Liv - ing thus I shall not per - ish, But shall live e - ter - nal - ly.

ACT OF SPIRITUAL COMMUNION. (Chant.)

GREGORIAN.

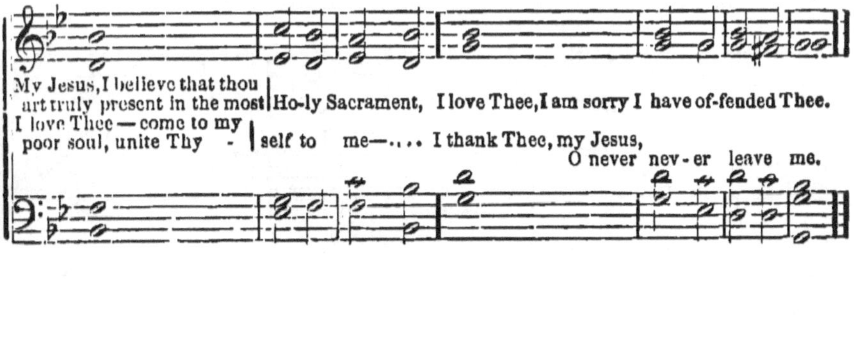

My Jesus, I believe that thou | Ho-ly Sacrament, I love Thee, I am sorry I have of-fended Thee.
art truly present in the most
I love Thee — come to my
poor soul, unite Thy — | self to me—.... I thank Thee, my Jesus,
                                           O never nev-er leave me.

HOLY COMMUNION.
DUET or TWO-PART CHORUS.

1. O dearest Lord, my life, my love! On Thee in prayer I humbly call, Come down to me from heav'n above! Thou art my food, my God, my all; my God, my all.
2. O when wilt Thou be always mine? And when will I be always thine? In life I shall adhere to Thee, In death be Thou support to me, support to me.
3. Within me do thou fix thy throne, That I may love but thee alone; Take full possession of my heart And from my soul do not depart, do not depart.
4. Lord Jesus, may I die in peace, To see thee ever face to face, In blissful kingdom there to dwell, Secure from Satan's sinful spell, his sinful spell.

Sweet Jesus, 'tis my fond desire To love but Thee till I expire, Sweet Jesus, 'tis my fond desire To love but Thee till I expire.

WHILE SHEPHERDS WATCHED.

[CHRISTMAS CAROL.]

Old English Air. Harm. by WM. F. TOMLINS.

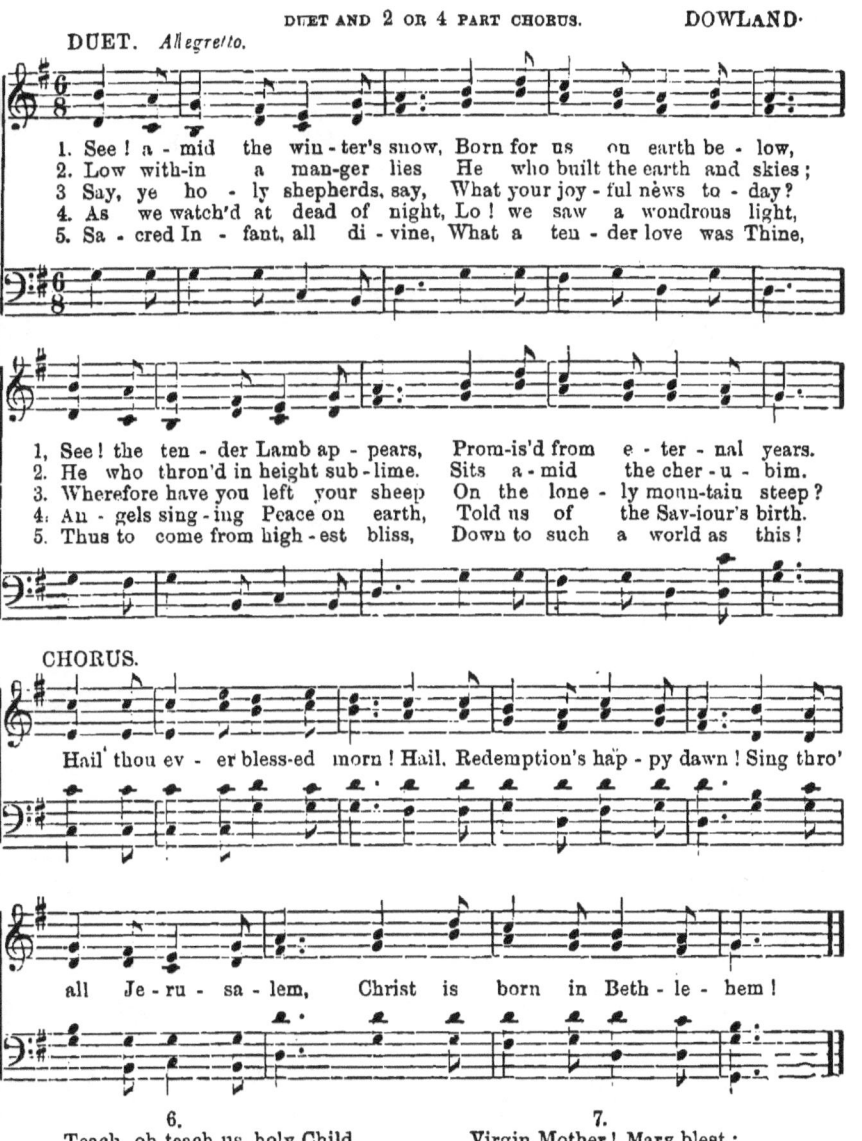

SEE! AMID THE WINTER'S SNOW.

DUET AND 2 OR 4 PART CHORUS.   DOWLAND.

1. See! a-mid the win-ter's snow, Born for us on earth be-low,
2. Low with-in a man-ger lies He who built the earth and skies;
3. Say, ye ho-ly shepherds, say, What your joy-ful news to-day?
4. As we watch'd at dead of night, Lo! we saw a wondrous light,
5. Sa-cred In-fant, all di-vine, What a ten-der love was Thine,

1. See! the ten-der Lamb ap-pears, Prom-is'd from e-ter-nal years.
2. He who thron'd in height sub-lime. Sits a-mid the cher-u-bim.
3. Wherefore have you left your sheep On the lone-ly moun-tain steep?
4. An-gels sing-ing Peace on earth, Told us of the Sav-iour's birth.
5. Thus to come from high-est bliss, Down to such a world as this!

CHORUS.

Hail' thou ev-er bless-ed morn! Hail. Redemption's hap-py dawn! Sing thro' all Je-ru-sa-lem, Christ is born in Beth-le-hem!

6.
Teach, oh teach us, holy Child,
By Thy face so meek and mild,
Teach us to resemble Thee
In Thy sweet humility! Cho.

7.
Virgin Mother! Mary blest;
By the joys that fill thy breast
Pray for us, that we may prove
Worthy of the Saviour's love.   Cho

"Adeste Fideles." No. 1. Concluded. 81

2 God to God equal,
   Light of Light eternal,
   Lo! he abhors not the Vir-
        [gin's womb.
   True God of true God,
   Begotten, not created.
        O come, etc.

3 Sing, choirs of angels,
   Sing in exultation;
   Sing, all ye citizens of Heav-
        [en above.
   Glory to God,
   Glory in the highest.
        O come, etc.

4 Yea, Lord, we greet thee,
   Born this happy morning;
   Jesus, to Thee be glory
        [given.
   Word of the Father,
   Now in flesh appearing.
        O come, etc.

Other Christmas Hymns and Carols are published in a little book entitled " Christmas Chimes." Price 30 cents, or $15 per hundred.

82. COME, ALL YE FAITHFUL. (Adeste Fideles No. 2.)

"Come, all ye Faithful." Concluded.

* If sung only by children, or female voices, these *four bars* may be omitted.
The English words may also be sung to the music of Adeste Fideles, No. 1.

2
Deum de Deo,
Lumen de Lumine,
Gestant puellæ viscera;
Deum verum,
Genitum non factum:
    Venite, etc.

3
Cantet nunc Io!
Chorus angelorum:
Cantet nunc aula cælestium,
Gloria, Gloria
In excelsis Deo.
    Venite, etc.

4
Ergo qui natus
Die hodierna,
Jesu tibi sit gloria.
Patris æterna
Verbum caro factum.
    Venite, etc.

LOVE OF JESUS.
DUET OR TWO-PART CHORUS.

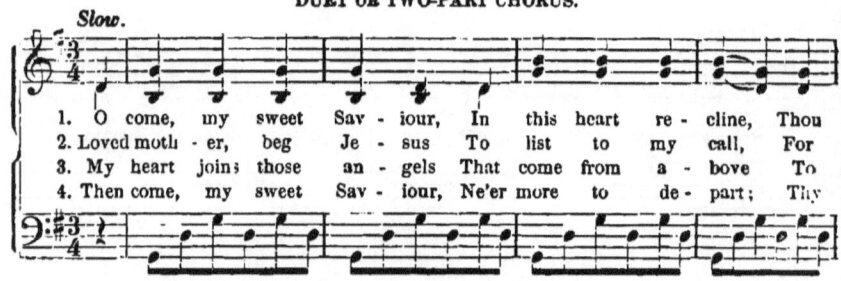

1. O come, my sweet Saviour, In this heart recline, Thou
2. Loved mother, beg Jesus To list to my call, For
3. My heart joins those angels That come from above To
4. Then come, my sweet Saviour, Ne'er more to depart; Thy

1 knowest, my Jesus, 'Twill ever be thine.
2 He is my Saviour, My God, and my all.
3 sing 'round this altar Hosannas of love.
4 home is my bosom, Thy altar my heart.

CHORUS.

O God of love, my soul's sweet delight, Keep

ever thy child From sin's dreary night.

SWEET HEART OF JESUS.
DUET & CHORUS.

Slow. With expression.

1. Sweet heart of Je - sus, source of love and mer - cy, We
2. Would that our hearts, re- spond-ing to thy longings, Were
3. Sweet heart of Je - sus, oh how much it grieves us, To
4. Look on our Pon - tiff, now so base-ly treated, Re-

1 beg of Thee, O fount of living grace, Oh, list to souls who humbly now im-
2 pure and sin - ple, seeking none but Thee; E'er self for- get - ting, patient, meek and
3 see Thy love so oft-en un - re-paid, To hear Thee scorn'd, derid - ed and re-
4 -store him to his rights and royal crown; O! make his sub - jects loyal and o-

1 -plore Thee, And make them thine for ev - er, ev - er more.
2 humble, And loving Thee with pure se - raph-ic love.
3 -jected, By those for whom Thy loving heart e'er yearns.
4 -bedient, As he e'er is to his great God and King.

CHORUS.

Sweet heart of Je - sus so hum - ble and so mild,

Sweet heart of Je - sus O make our hearts all Thine.

HEART OF JESUS OUR HOME.

THREE-PART CHORUS.

1. O Sacred Heart! Our home lies deep in thee! On earth thou art an exile's rest, In Heav'n the glory of the blest.
2. O Sacred Heart! Thou fount of contrite tears! Where-e'er those living waters flow, New life to sinners they bestow.
3. O Sacred Heart! Our trust is all in thee! For though earth's night be dark and drear, Thou breathest rest when thou art near.
4. O Sacred Heart! When shades of death shall fall, Receive us 'neath Thy gentle care, And save us from the tempter's snare.
5. O Sacred Heart! Lead exiled children home, Where we may ever rest near thee In peace and joy eternally.

CHORUS.

Sweet Sacred Heart! we thee implore, Make us love thee more and more.

JESUS CRUCIFIED.

DUET or MIXED QUARTET.

1. O come and mourn with me a-while, See Ma-ry calls us to her side; O come and let us mourn with her, Je-sus, our love, is cru-ci-fied! Have we no tears to shed for Him, While sol-diers scoff and Jews de-ride? Ah! look how pa-tient-ly he hangs, Je-sus, our love, is cru-ci-fied!

2. How fast his Hands and Feet are nail'd; His blessed Tongue with thirst is tied, His fail-ing Eyes are blind with blood, Je-sus, our love, is cru-ci-fied! His mother can-not reach his Face, She stands in help-less-ness be-side, Her heart is martyr'd with her Son's, Je-sus, our love, is cru-ci-fied!

3. Seven times He spoke seven words of love, And all three hours his silence cried For mer-cy on the souls of men, Je-sus, our love, is cru-ci-fied! What was thy crime, my dearest Lord? By earth, by heav'n thou hast been tried, And guilt-y found of too much love, Je-sus, our love, is cru-ci-fied!

4. Found guilt-y of ex-cess of love, It was thine own sweet will that tied Thee tight-er far than helpless nails; Je-sus, our love, is cru-ci-fied! Death came, and Je-sus meekly bowed, His fail-ing Eyes He strove to guide With mind-ful love to Ma-ry's face;— Je-sus, our love, is cru-ci-fied!

AVE MARIA. No. 1.

DUET or TWO-PART CHORUS.

1 ple - na, A - ve, Ma - ri - a, A - ve Ma - ri - a.
2 De - i, Sanc - ta Ma - ri - a, O - ra pro no - bis.

AVE MARIA. No. 2.

DUET OR TWO-PART CHORUS.

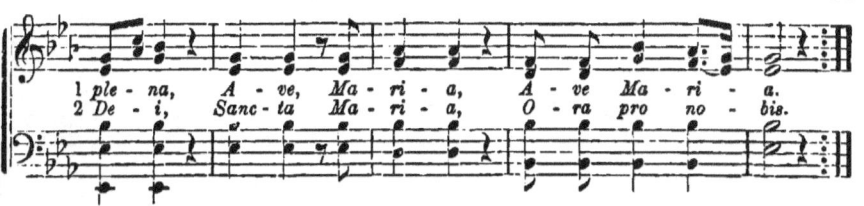

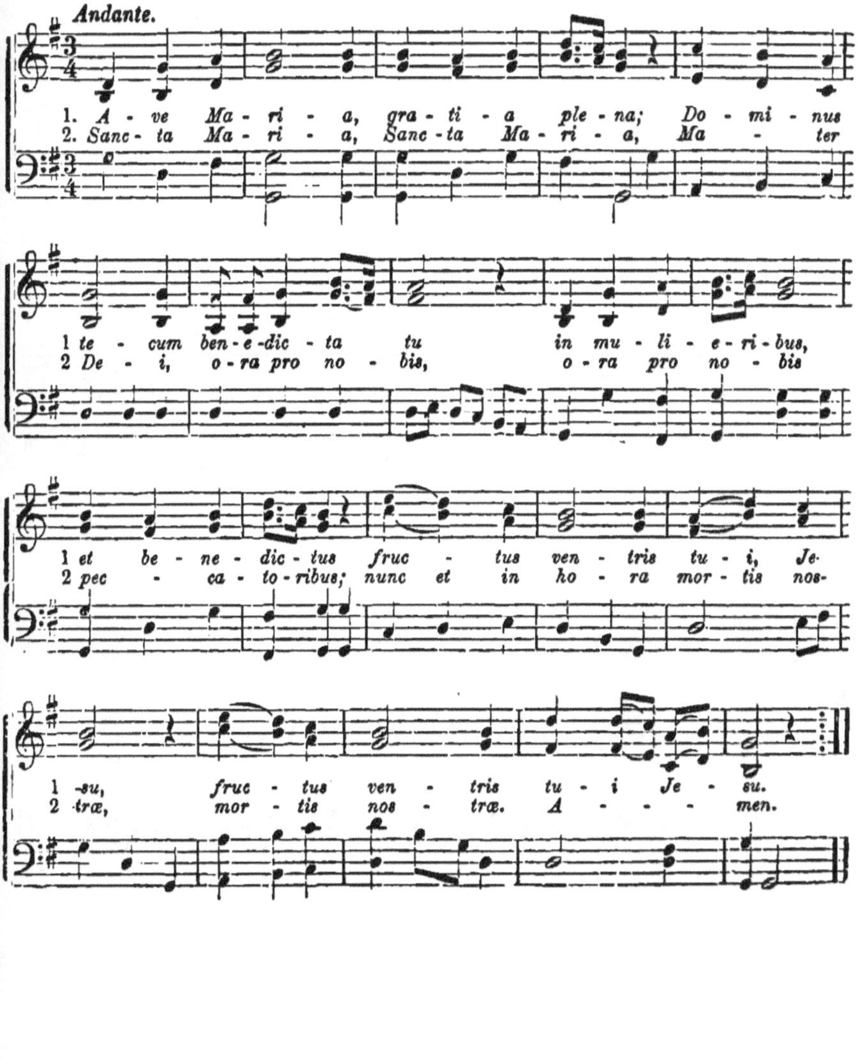
Andante.
1. A - ve Ma - ri - a, gra - ti - a ple - na; Do - mi - nus
2. Sanc - ta Ma - ri - a, Sanc - ta Ma - ri - a, Ma - ter
1 te - cum ben - e - dic - ta tu in mu - li - e - ri - bus,
2 De - i, o - ra pro no - bis, o - ra pro no - bis
1 et be - ne - dic - tus fruc - tus ven - tris tu - i, Je-
2 pec - ca - to - ribus; nunc et in ho - ra mor - tis nos-
1 -su, fruc - tus ven - tris tu - i Je - su.
2 -træ, mor - tis nos - træ. A - - - - men.

GENTLE STAR OF OCEAN. (Ave Maris Stella. No. 3.)

DUET or TWO-PART CHORUS.

A - ve Ma - ris Stel - la, De - i Ma - ter al - ma, Atque

1. Gen - tle Star of O - cean, Por - tal of the sky, Ever
2. Oh! by Ga - bri - el's A - ve, Ut - ter'd long a - go, Eva's
3. Break the cap - tive's fet - ters; Light on blind - ness pour; All our
4. Show thy - self a Moth - er; Of - fer Him our sighs, Who for
5. Vir - gin of all Vir - gins! to thy care us take; Gentlest
6. Still as on we jour - ney, Help us in our choice; Till with

sem - per Vir - go, Fe - lix cœ-li por - ta. CHORUS.

1 Vir - gin Mother, Of the Lord most high.
2 name re - versing, 'Stablish peace be - low.
3 ills ex - pelling, Ev - 'ry bliss im-plore.
4 us In - carnate, Did not thee despise.
5 of the gentle! Chaste and gentle us make.
6 Thee and Jesus, Ev - er we re - joice.

E - vi - va Ma - ri - a! Ma-

-ri - a, E - vi - va E - vi - va Ma - ri - a! E chi la cre - o.

"Our Lady of Help." Concluded.

CHORUS.

Our Mother pure and holy, Will lend us aid from above; Let earth repeat the story, And join our hymn of love, And join our hymn of love, And join our hymn of love.

O SANCTISSIMA.

1. O Sanctissima, O purissima, Dulcis Virgo Maria,
2. Tota pulchra es, O Maria! Et macula non est in te,
3. Sicut lilium, Inter spinus, Sic Maria inter filius,

Mater amata, intemerata, Ora, Ora pro nobis.

HEART OF MARY.
DUET & TWO-PART CHORUS.

5 As children to their mother flee
 When storm-clouds is darkly lower,
So loving hearts will haste to thee
 In sad affliction's hour.

6 As doves all innocent and pure
 Repose within their nest,
So we from every ill secure
 In Mary's Heart shall rest.

7 Sweet Heart, within thy depths so chaste
 We'll dwell and ne'er depart,
Till thou our souls hast deeply placed
 In Jesus' Sacred Heart.

8 And when from the loved heart we'll go,
 To that of thy dear Son,
O shall we leave thee then — Ah no.
 His Heart and thine are one.

SWEET LADY.

SOLO & CHORUS.

Slow.

1. Sweet La-dy of the Sacred Heart, Thy peerless Virgin charms Wooed
2. Sweet La-dy of the Sacred Heart, What joy thy bosom filled, When
3. Sweet La-dy of the Sacred Heart, From Je-sus' opened side, On
4. Sweet La-dy of the Sacred Heart, Proclaim thy power a-bove, From
5. Sweet La-dy of the Sacred Heart, When death with i-cy hand, Lays
6. Sweet La-dy of the Sacred Heart, If thou wilt hov-er near, Death's

1 Je-sus from His heav'nly throne To rest with-in thine arms, Wooed
2 close to thine thy In-fant's heart In gen-tle puls-es thrilled, When
3 thee the wa-ter and the blood Flowed as a sav-ing tide, On
4 Je-sus' wounds send piercing darts, Trans-fix our souls with love, From
5 on our frighted hearts his touch, O! Ma-ry, near us stand, Lays
6 deepest shades in thy clear light Will quick-ly dis-ap-pear, Death's

CHORUS.

1 Je-sus from His heav'nly throne, To rest with-in thine arms. Sweet
2 close to thine thy In-fant's heart, In gen-tle puls-es thrilled. Sweet
3 thee the wa-ter and the blood, Flowed as a sav-ing tide. Sweet
4 Je-sus' wounds send piercing darts, Trans-fix our souls with love. Sweet
5 on our frighted hearts his touch, O! Ma-ry, near us stand. Sweet
6 deep-est shades in thy clear light, Will quickly dis-ap-pear. Sweet

La-dy, sweet La-dy, Sweet La-dy of the Sa-cred Heart.

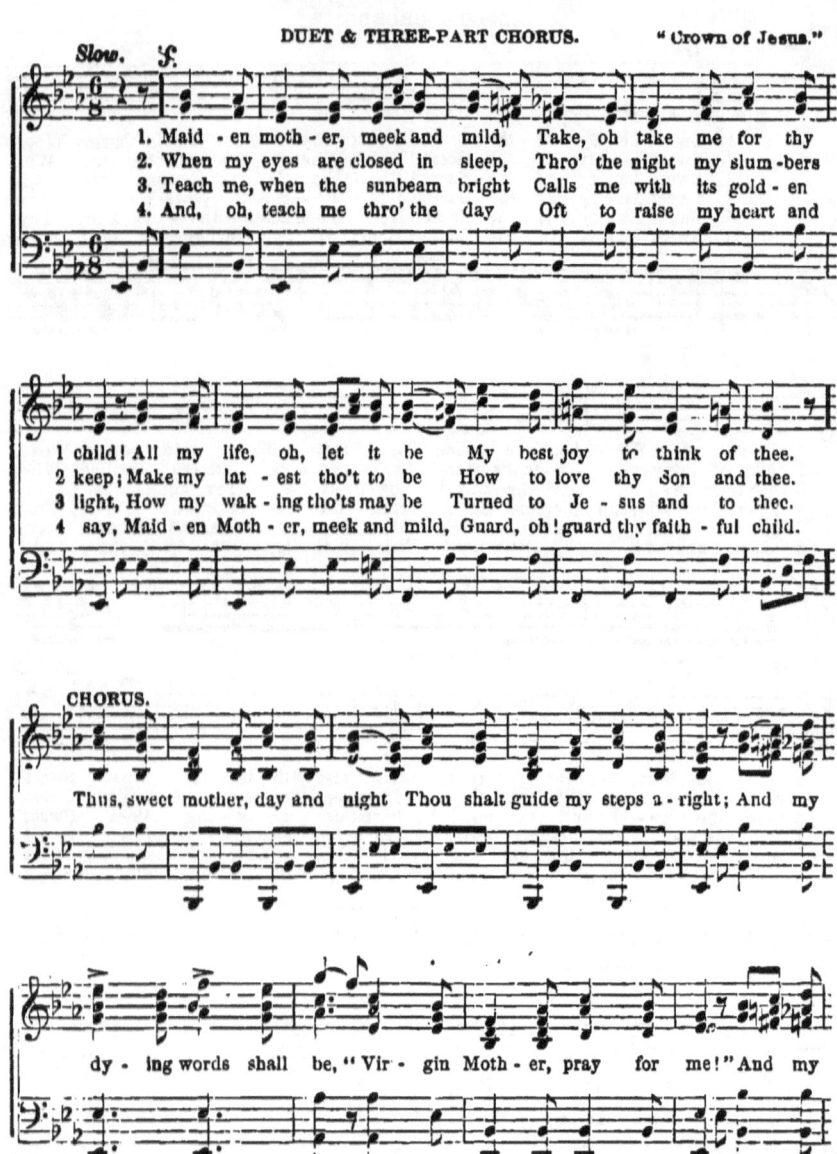

"Maiden Mother." Concluded.

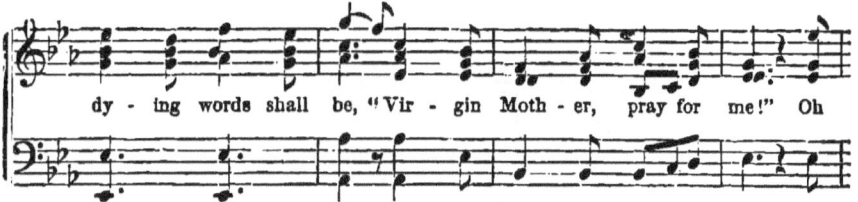

dy - ing words shall be, "Vir - gin Moth - er, pray for me!" Oh

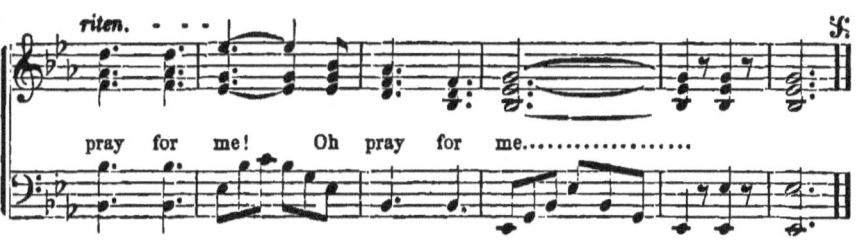

riten.

pray for me! Oh pray for me..............

O MARY BLEST.

HEMY. "Crown of Jesus."

Moderato.

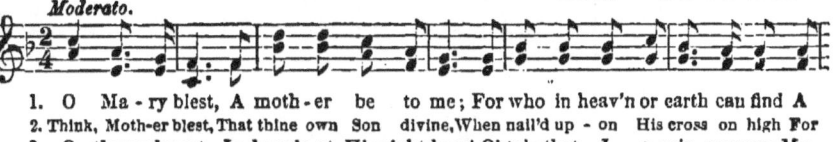

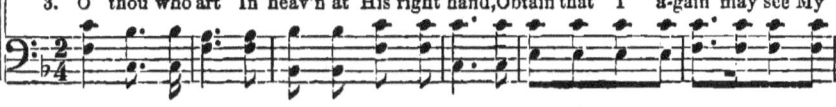

1. O Ma - ry blest, A moth - er be to me; For who in heav'n or earth can find A
2. Think, Moth-er blest, That thine own Son divine, When nail'd up - on His cross on high For
3. O thou who art In heav'n at His right hand, Obtain that I a - gain may see My

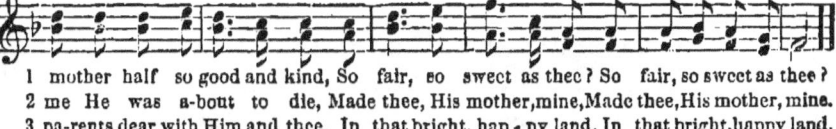

1 mother half so good and kind, So fair, so sweet as thee? So fair, so sweet as thee?
2 me He was a-bout to die, Made thee, His mother, mine, Made thee, His mother, mine.
3 pa-rents dear with Him and thee, In that bright, hap - py land, In that bright, happy land.

"Mother Loved." Concluded.

1. O Mother loved, watch o-ver me, So helpless, I tossed on life's rough sea; Kindly shed from heaven a-bove A Mother's sweet fond smile of love.
2. O Mother loved, watch o-ver me, From sin and danger keep me free; When temptation's waves angry flow, Thyself to me a Mother show.
3. O Mother loved, watch o-ver me, When life is bright and fair to see; Who so need thy clear guiding ray As those that walk the flow'ry way.

"Mary, Mother Sweet." Concluded.

CHORUS.

Ma - ry, Moth - er sweet, Ma - ry, Moth - er fair, Vir - gin Queen of May, hear our prayer! Un - to Je - sus pray that each day We may grow like thee, Our Queen of May.

D. C.

O SANCTISSIMA.

SICILIAN.

1. O Sanc - tis - si - ma, O pu - ris - si - ma, Dul - cis Vir - go Ma - ri - a,
2. To - ta pulchra es, O Ma - ri - a! Et ma - cu - la non est in - te,
3. Si - cut li - li - um, In - ter spi - nas, Sic Ma - ria in - ter fi - li - us,

Ma - ter a - mata, in - te - me - ra - ta, O - ra, O - ra pro no - bis.

HAIL, VIRGIN! DEAREST MARY! (May Hymn.)

JOY OF MY HEART.
MAY HYMN.
TRIO WITH BASS AD LIB. — LAMBILLOTTE.

1. Joy of my heart! O let me pay To thee thine own sweet
2. Thou, Mary, art my hope and life, The star-light of this
3. Thou who wert pure as driv-en snow, Make me as thou wert
4. Write on my heart's most se-cret core, The five dear wounds that

month of May; Ma-ry, one gift I beg of thee,
earth-ly strife. Sweet Day-Star! let thy beau-ty be
here be-low; Oh! Queen of Heaven! ob-tain for me
Je-sus bore, O give me tears to shed with thee,

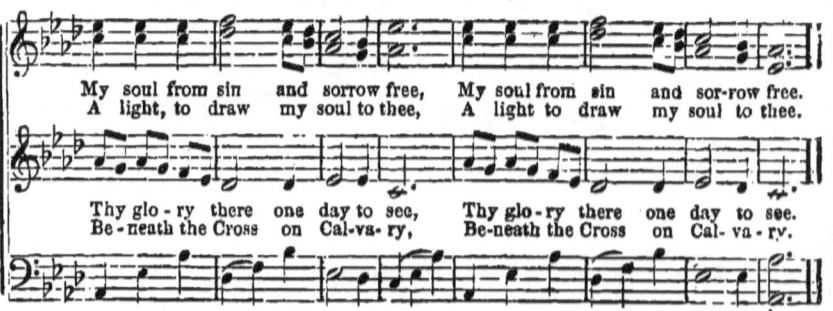

My soul from sin and sorrow free, My soul from sin and sor-row free,
A light, to draw my soul to thee, A light to draw my soul to thee.
Thy glo-ry there one day to see, Thy glo-ry there one day to see.
Be-neath the Cross on Cal-va-ry, Be-neath the Cross on Cal-va-ry.

No. 11. OUR QUEEN IMMACULATE.

SOLO & TWO-PART CHORUS.

Arranged from AVE MARIA

SOLO.

1. Oh fair - est of all vis - ions, With meek - ly fold - ed hands, A-
2. Oh fair - est of all vis - ions, That met the ea - ger gaze Of
3. Ex - pec - tant yet for a - ges, That earth must yet a - wait, Fair
4. The King looked on thy beau - ty, In thy un - fall - en state, The
5. Oh fair - est of all vis - ions, En - tranc - ing mor - tal eyes; The
6. Oh fair - est of all vis - ions, Our wea - ry ex - ile o'er, In
7. We'll see thee Queen and Moth - er, Enthroned in roy - al state, In

1 -dor - ing eyes up - lift - ed, Be - fore her God she stands.
2 Pa - tri - arch and pro - phet, In far pri - me - val days.
3 Sha - ron's Rose, God's moth - er, Our Queen Im - mac - u - late.
4 Spir - it's Bride, the Vir - gin, Our Queen Im - mac - u - late.
5 veil is half up - lift - ed, We gaze in fond sur - prise.
6 thy un - cloud - ed glo - ry We'll see thee ev - er - more.
7 all thy vir - gin splen - dor, Our Queen Im - mac - u - late.

CHORUS.

Mother pure, Virgin fair, Spotless Dove, Peerless maid,

Mother pure, Virgin fair, Spotless Dove, Peerless maid, Crowned

Queen of God's cre - a - tion, Our Queen Im - mac - u - late.

Rall.

AVE MARIA, GUARDIAN DEAR. (Evening Hymn.)

THREE-PART CHORUS & DUET.

LAMBILLOTTE.

"Ave Maria, Guardian Dear." Concluded

1 ray   Wake a - gain our an - them sound.
2 Child, Hear the prayer we raise to thee!
3 tomb, Shine up - on the des - ert there.

AS THE DEWY SHADES OF EVEN.

Evening Hymn to the Blessed Virgin Mary.
DUET or QUARTET.

Grazioso.   LAMBILLOTTE.

1. As the dew - y shades of ev - en   Gath - er
2. Ho - ly Moth-er! near me hov - er, Free my
3. Thine own sin - less heart was bro - ken, Sor - row's
4. Queen of heav - en, guard and guide me, Save my

1 o'er the balm - y air,   Lis - ten, gen - tle
2 thoughts from ought de - filed;   With thy wings of
3 sword had pierced its core;   Ho - ly Moth - er,
4 soul from dark de - spair;   In thy ten - der

1 Queen of Heav - en, Lis - ten to our Ves - per prayer.
2 mer - cy cov - er, Keep from sin thy help - less child.
3 by that to - ken Now thy pi - ty I im - plore.
4 bo - som hide me, Take me, Moth - er to thy care.

5
Hail! holy Joseph, hail!
Teach us our flesh to tame;
And, Mary, keep the hearts
That love Saint Joseph's name.
Hail, etc.

6
Mother of Jesus! bless,
And bless, ye saints on high,
All meek and simple souls
That to Saint Joseph cry.
Hail, etc.

HYMN TO ST. PATRICK.
DUET OR QUARTET.

"St. Aloysius." Concluded.

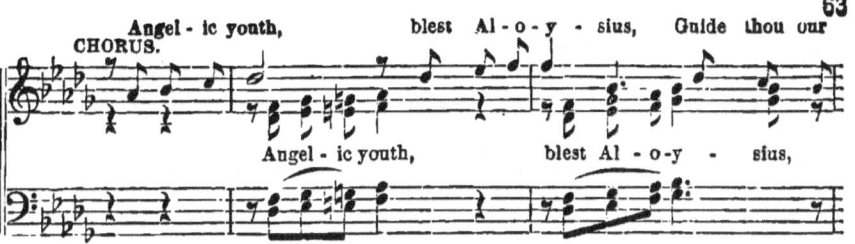

PETERS' SODALITY HYMN-BOOK,

COMPILED AND ARRANGED
BY THE
SISTERS OF NOTRE DAME, CINCINNATI O.

Price, in Paper, 35 cts.; $3.60 per dozen. In Boards, 40 cts.; $4 per dozen.

CONTENTS.

	PAGE
Act of Contrition, (O God, have mercy.) Chant,	4
Act of Desire, (Come, sweet Jesus.)....... Mozart,	75
Act of Faith, (In this Sacrament.) .... Mozart,	75
Act of Spiritual Communion, (My Jesus, I believe.)	75
Adeste fideles, No. 1, (O come, all ye faithful.) Christmas Hymn. 2 or 4 voices..... Portuguese,	80
Adeste fideles, No. 2 .... Lerler,	82
Adoro te supplex. For Offertory or Benediction,	24
Advent Hymn, (Come, O divine Messiah.) Duet or 2-part Chorus.............. Lambillotte,	62
Advent Hymn, for Vespers, (Creator alme s.d run.)	63
Again the Holy morn,(Morning Hymn.).... Hays,	96
Agnus Dei. Of short Choral Mass in E♭. 2 or 4 voices .... German,	21
Agnus Dei. Of short Choral Requiem Mass in E Minor. 2 or 4 voices......... Wm. Dressler,	34
Alma Redemptoris. Antiphon of the B. V. from Advent to Purification. 2-part Chorus.... Goria,	54
Annunciation, (The,) (How pure.) Solo and Duet or 2-part Chorus...... Sisters of Notre Dame,	102
Antiphons of the B. V. M. Alma, p. 54; Ave Regina, p. 55; Salve, p. 56; Regina cœli......	57
Asperges me. Antiphon and Psalm sung before Mass .... Arranged from the Gregorian,	6
As the dewy shades. Evening Hymn. Duet or Quartet............. .... Lambillotte,	119
As the gentle Spring, (Mary, Mother sweet.) May Hymn. Duet or 2-part Chorus... Concone,	112
Ave Maria, No. 1, in E♭. Duet or 2-part Chorus,	94
Ave Maria, No. 2, in G. Duet or 2-part Chorus..	95
Ave Maria, bright and pure, (Ora pro me.) Duet. Sisters of Notre Dame,	103
Ave Maria, Guardian dear. Evening Hymn. Duet, Chorus and Duet.............. Lambillotte,	118
Ave Maris Stella, No. 1. Vesper Hymn and Responses for Feasts of the B. V. M.... Srs. N. D.,	60
Ave Maris Stella, No. 2. Duet....... Blumenthal,	61
Ave Maris Stella, No. 3, (Gentle Star of Ocean.)	98
Ave Regina. Antiphon of the B. V. M., from Purification to Easter. Solo and 3-part Cho. Weber,	55
Ave Verum. For Off. or Ben. Duet and Chorus,	26
Beatus vir. Psalm 111, Com. Vespers. Gregorian,	46
Benedictus. Of short Choral Mass..... German,	20
Benedictus. Of short Choral Requiem Mass. 2 or 4 voices .... Wm. Dressler,	32
Christmas Carol, (While Shepherds watched their flocks.) 2 or 4 voices.............. Tomlins,	78
Christmas Hymn, (Holy Church, thou art our Mother. 2 or 4 part Chorus .. .. Dowland,	79
Christmas Hymn, Adeste fideles, No. 1, (O come, all ye faithful.) 2 or 4 voices..... Portuguese,	80
Christmas Hymn, Adeste fideles, No. 2.... Lerler,	82
Christmas Hymn for Vespers, (Jesu Redemptor Omnium.) 2 or 4 voices............ Westlake,	64
Christian Soul, dost thou desire, (The yoke of Christ.) Suitable for Funerals. 2 or 4 v... Pleyel,	41

	PAGE
Come, Creator Spirit blest, (Veni Creator, Nos. 1 and 2.) Sung before a Sermon. Duet or Quartet,	13
Come, O Divine Messiah, (Hymn for Advent.) Duet or 2-part Chorus............. Lambillotte,	62
Come, sweet Jesus, (Act of Desire.)..... Mozart,	75
Confitebor. Psalm 110, Com. Vespers.. Gregorian,	46
Creator alme siderum. Vesper Hymn for the Sundays in Advent. Duet or 2-pt. Cho... Gregorian,	63
Credo. Of short Choral Mass in E♭..... German,	14
Dear Angel, ever at my side, (Hymn to my Angel Guardian. Duet or Quartet....	121
Dear little one, how sweet thou art, (Hymn to the Infant Jesus.) Dt. or 2-pt. Cho., or Quar.. Hays,	84
De Profundis. (Psalm 129) For Funerals or Penitential occasions. Chant............ Gregorian,	37
Desire of Heaven, (When I am taken from this world.) Suitable for Funerals. Dt. and 2-pt. Cho.,	40
Dies Iræ, (Sequence from short Choral Requiem Mass in E Minor.) 2 or 4 voices. Wm. Dressler,	29
Dixit Dominus. Psalm 109 of Common Vespers,	44
Domine ad adjuvandum. Of Common Vespers,	44
Domine Jesu Christe. Offertory of short Choral Requiem Mass................. Wm. Dressler,	31
Evening Hymn, (Hail, holy Queen.) ...Dressler,	120
Evening Hymn, (As the dewy shades.) Duet and Quartet .... Lambillotte,	119
Evening Hymn, (Ave Maria, Guardian dear.)	118
Eve of Communion, (To-morrow morn.) Duet and 2-part Chorus..................... Lambillotte,	74
Funeral Mass. Short Choral Requiem Mass complete, in E♭. 2 or 4 voices....... Wm. Dressler,	28
Funeral Hymns..... ...Pages 37, 38, 40, 41, 42, 43,	99
Gentle Star of Ocean, (Ave Maris Stella, No. 3,)	98
Gloria. Of short Choral Mass, in E♭............	11
God of Might. 2 voices and Bass ad lib...German,	77
Hail! Holy Joseph, hail. Duet...... Lambillotte,	122
Hail! Holy Queen. Evening Hymn.... Dressler,	120
Hail! Mary. Chant. 4 voices........ Gregorian,	4
Hail, Patron of Erin, (Hymn to St. Patrick.) Duet or Quartet................... Raphaelson,	125
Hail! Queen of Heaven. Duet or mixed Quartet,	100
Hail! Virgin, dearest Mary, (May Hymn).......	114
Heart of the Holy Child. Duet... Wm. Dressler,	85
Heart of Jesus our home, (O Sacred Heart).	91
Heart of Mary, (O Heart of Mary.) Duet or Cho.,	106
Heavenly desire, (Oh! when shall we with angels bright.) Duet.......... Sisters of Notre Dame,	99
Holy Church, thou art our Mother. 2 or 4 voices,	5
Holy Communion, (O dearest Lord.) Duet or Cho.,	76
Holy Mary, Mother mild. Solo and Cho.. Dressler,	101
Holy Name of Jesus, (Jesus, the only thought,)	86
How pure, how frail and white, (The Annunciation.) Solo and Duet, or 2-part Chorus..... Srs. N. D.,	102
Hymn to my Angel Guardian, (Dear angel, ever at my side.) Duet or Quartet	121
Hymns for Benediction, pages 24, 25, 65, 66, 67, 68,	69

CONTENTS PETERS' SODALITY HYMN-BOOK.—Continued.

	PAGE
Hymns to the B. V. M., pages 4, 52–61, 94, 95, 98–120	
Hymns suitable for Offertories, pages 18, 24, 25, 65, 94, 95	
Hymns to Saints................ pages 121 to 126	
Hymns suitable for Funerals, pages 37, 38, 40, 41, 42, 43, 99	
Hymns for the Month of May...... pages 112, 114, 116	
Hymns for Christmas ....pages 64, 78, 79, 80, 82	
Hymns for Advent........ ....pages 54, 62, 63	
Hymns for Lent........ ....pages 37, 38, 55, 93	
In exitu in Israel. Psalm 113 of Common Vespers,	48
In this sweet Sacrament, (Act of Faith).....Mozart,	75
I want to be an Angel. Solo and Cho...Dressler,	97
Jesus crucified. (O, come and mourn.) Duet.....	93
Jesus, my God, my all, (O Jesus, Jesus, dearest Lord.) Duet or mixed Quartet........Dressler,	89
Jesu Redemptor omnium, (Vesper Hymn for Christmas Day.) 2 or 4 voices ....Westlake,	64
Jesus, the only thought of Thee, (Holy Name of Jesus.) Solo and 3-part Chorus..............	86
Joy of my heart, (May Hymn).......Lambillotte,	116
Kyrie eleison, (of short Choral Mass, in E♭)German,	10
Kyrie eleison, (Choral Requiem Mass)...Dressler,	28
Kyrie eleison. Litany of the B. V., No. 1..Wesley,	70
Kyrie eleison. Litany of the B. V., No. 2	72
Lætatus sum. Psalm 121. (Vespers of the B. V. M.)	58
Lauda Jerusalem. Psalm 147, Vespers of the B. V. M.) Chant.....................Gregorian,	58
Laudate Dominum in sanctis ejus. Chant..Greg'n,	3
Laudate Dominum omnes gentes. Psalm 116....	50
Laudate pueri Dominum. Ps. 112. Chant..Greg'n,	48
Libera me Domine, (of short Choral Requiem Mass ....Wm. Dressler,	36
Litany of the B. V. M., No. 1...........Wesley,	70
Litany of the B. V. M. Nos. 2, 3, and 4..........	72
Lucis Creator optime, Nos. 1 and 2, (O great Creator of the Light.) Vesper Hymn for Sundays..	51
Love of Jesus (O come, my sweet Saviour.) Duet,	83
Magnificat, (Canticle of the B. V. M.,) of Common Vespers. Chant..............Gregorian	52
Maiden Mother. Duet and Cho....Crown of Jesus,	108
Mary, hear my fervent prayer, (Mother loved.)	110
Mary, Mother sweet, (As the gentle Spring.) May Hymn. Duet and 2-part Chorus....Concone,	112
Mass, short Choral, in E♭, complete. 2 or 4 voices,	10
Mass for the Dead. Short Choral Requiem in E Minor, complete... .... Wm. Dressler,	27
May Hymns............ ......pages 112, 114, 116	
Miserere. Psalm 50, for Funerals and Penitential occasions. Chant...............Gregorian,	38
Morning Hymn, (Again this holy morn).. Hays,	96
Mother loved, (Mary, hear my fervent prayer.) Dt. or 2-part Chorus and Solo..........Lambillotte,	110
My Jesus, I believe, (Act of Spiritual Communion,)	75
Nisi Dominus. Psalm 126, Vespers of B. V. M.,	58
O! Christians of sincere, (Our Lady of Help.)	104
O come and mourn, (Jesus crucified.) For Lent,	93
O come, all ye faithful, (Adeste fideles, No. 1.)...	80
O come, all ye faithful, (Adeste fideles, No. 2.)....	82
O come, my sweet Saviour, (Love of Jesus.) Duet,	83
O dearest Lord. (Holy Communion.) Duet or Cho.,	76
Oh! fairest of all visions, (Our Queen immaculate.) Solo and 2-part Chorus............."	
Offertory, (Hymns suitable for,) pages 18, 24, 25, 65, 94, 95	
Offertory, (O Jesu Deus.) Choral Mass..Dressler,	18
Offertory. Of Requiem Mass, (Domine Jesu Christe.) .... Wm. Dressler,	
O God, have mercy, (Act of contrition.) Chant,	4
O Great Creator of the Light, (Lucis Creator,) Nos. 1 and 2. Vesper Hymn for Sundays. 2 or 4 v.,	51
O Heart of Mary, (Heart of Mary.) Dt. or 2-pt Ch.	106

	PAGE
O Jesu Deus. Offertory. Duet........Dressler,	18
O Jesus dear, (Sacred Heart.) 2-part Cho. and Dt.,	92
O Jesus, dearest, (Jesus, my God, my all)..Dressler,	89
O Mary blest. 2 or 4 voices......Crown of Jesus,	109
Ora pro me, (Ave Maria.) Sisters of Notre Dame,	103
O Sacred Heart, (Heart of Jesus our home.) Cho.,	91
O Salutaris. For Off. or Ben. 2 v. and Bass ad lib.,	65
O Sanctissima, (Hymn to the B. V. M.).. Cramer,	105
O Sanctissima, No. 2 2 v. and Bass ad lib. Sicilian	113
O! thou, on whose bright natal day, (Hymn to St. Aloysius.) Duet and Chorus.......Lambillotte,	124
O! when shall we with angels bright, (Heavenly desire.) Duet ......Sisters of Notre Dame,	99
Our Father. Chant...................Gregorian.	4
Our Lady of Help, (Oh! Christian of sincere.)	104
Our Queen immaculate, (Oh! fairest of all visions,)	117
Panis angelicus. For Off. or Ben. Tr. Lambillotte,	25
Pie Jesu. Choral Requiem Mass...Wm. Dressler,	33
Pray for the Dead. 2 or 4 voices...Wm. Dressler,	43
Regina cœli. Antiphon of the B. V. M....	56
Requiem æternam. Requiem Mass. Wm. Dressler,	27
Responses after Asperges me and Vidi aquam....	7
Responses after Ave Maris Stella, Feasts B. V. M.,	60
Responses after Litany to the B. V. M.........	70
Responses after the 4 Antiphons of the B. V. M. Pages 54, 55, 56,	57
Responses after Requiem Mass.................	37
Responses at High Mass......................	22
Responses at Vespers.................50, 51, 52	
Responses after Tantum ergo..................	66
Sacred heart, (O Jesus dear,) 2-pt. Cho. and Duet,	92
Salve Regina. Antiphon of the B. V. M.	57
Sanctus. Of short Choral Mass.....	19
Sanctus. Of short Requiem Mass..............	32
See amid the winter's snow. Christmas Hymn.	79
Short Choral Mass, complete, in E♭.....German,	10
Short Choral Requiem Mass in E Minor, complete, for 2 or 4 voices..................Wm. Dressler,	27
St. Aloysius, (Hymn to.) Oh! thou, on whose bright natal day. Duet and Chorus..Lambillotte,	124
St. Agatha, (Hymn to.) We come to thee. Duet and 2 or 4-part Chorus...............Dressler,	126
St. Joseph, (Hymn to.) Hail, holy Joseph. Duet or 2-part Chorus.................Lambillotte,	122
St. Patrick, (Hymn to.) Hail, Patron of Erin. Duet or Quartet...............Raphaelson,	123
Sweet Heart of Jesus. Duet and Chorus..........	90
Sweet Lady of the Sacred Heart. Solo and Chorus,	107
Take me, my Jesus. Suitable for Funerals. Duet,	42
Tantum ergo, No. 1, in B♭. 3-pt. Cho. and Resp's,	66
Tantum ergo, No. 2, in F. 3-part Chorus.........	67
Tantum ergo, No. 3, in E♭. Duet or 2-part Chorus.	68
Te Deum. Sung at Benediction on occasions of Thanksgiving. Chant............Gregorian,	69
The Yoke of Christ, (Christian soul.) Suitable for Funerals. 2 or 4 voices ....Pleyel,	41
To-morrow morn, (Eve of Communion.) Duet....	74
Veni Creator, Nos. 1 and 2, (Come, Creator Spirit,)	13
Vespers, Common, for Sundays, complete......	44
Vespers, of the Blessed Virgin	58
Vidi Aquam. Antiphon and Psalm sung before Mass from Easter till Whitsunday....Dressler,	8
We come to thee. Hymn to St. Agatha..Dressler,	126
When I am taken from this world, (Desire of Heaven.) Suitable for Funerals. Dt. and 2-pt Ch.	40
While Shepherds watched their flocks. Christmas Carol. 2 or 4 voices .... Tomlins,	78
Yoke (The) of Christ, (Christian soul.) Suitable for Funerals. 2 or 4 voices........... Pleyel,	41

Valuable Music Books for Schools,
PUBLISHED BY
Oliver Ditson & Co., Boston, C. H. Ditson & Co., New York.

Either Book mailed, post-paid, for Retail Price.

AMERICAN SCHOOL MUSIC READERS.

By L. O. EMERSON and W. S. TILDEN. In Three Books.

These Music Readers are well fitted for use in connection with the new and improved methods of teaching music by note in schools.

The theoretic part has been prepared by Mr. W. S. TILDEN, who has had valuable experience as Music Teacher in the schools of Boston and vicinity.

In **Book I**, which is for Primary Schools, we have a three years' course of study very plainly laid out, with abundant directions to teachers, and a large number of sweet songs for the little ones to sing by rote and by note. Price 35 cents.

In **Book II**, the course above indicated is continued, and becomes a little more theoretic. The book is fitted for the use of the younger scholars in Grammar Schools. Price 50

In **Book III**, part singing is introduced, and the ear is trained to harmonic singing. For higher classes in Grammar Schools. Price 50 cents.

HOUR OF SINGING.

By L. O. EMERSON and W. S. TILDEN. For High Schools. Price $1.00.

Until recently, it could not be said that there was really any music book especially adapted for High Schools. There were, to be sure, excellent collections of music which could, after a fashion, be used in teaching. Still the instructor in Music had no proper text-book until the appearance of the "Hour of Singing." Its adaptedness to its place and work was so apparent, that it was at once, without question, adopted in a large number of High Schools and Seminaries; and has also, to a certain extent, been used by the higher classes of Grammar Schools.

THE HIGH SCHOOL CHOIR.

By L. O. EMERSON and W. S. TILDEN. Price $1.00. $9.00 per dozen.

The "High School Choir" is similar, in general design, to the very popular "Hour of Singing," which has been almost universally used in High Schools. The present work is in no way inferior to its predecessor, is entirely fresh and new, and is received with decided favor.

CHOICE TRIOS.

For Female Voices. By W. S. TILDEN. Price $1.00.

The music is all of a high order, is not very difficult, and excellently selected and arranged for High Schools, Seminaries, Academies, &c.

Collections of School Songs.

CHEERFUL VOICES.

By L. O. EMERSON. Price 50 cents.

The book contains a well written Elementary Course, with abundance of agreeable exercises and tunes for practice; and also a large and varied collection of Songs, Rounds, &c., with thirty pieces of Sacred Music for opening and closing school.

MERRY CHIMES.

By L. O. EMERSON. Price 50 cents.

Has an excellent reputation among School Song Books.

THE GOLDEN WREATH.

By L. O. EMERSON. Price 50 cents.

The success of this fine book has been a surprise, *more than a quarter of a million copies* having been sold. To that number of persons, therefore, its face is as that of a familiar friend.

THE NIGHTINGALE.

By W. O. & H. S. PERKINS. Price 50 cts.

A very appropriate name for a favorite collection of School Songs.

THE GOLDEN ROBIN.

By W. O. PERKINS. Price 50 cents.

Well chosen and good songs; more than two hundred of them; and the usual elementary course, with attractive exercises.

Cantatas for School Exhibitions.

Musical progress, both among young and old people, depends so much upon musical enthusiasm, that there seems to be almost a necessity for introducing Concerts and Exhibitions into the music-teaching course of schools. To give brilliancy and success to these affairs, nothing can be better than such Cantatas as are mentioned below:

The Flower Queen.	G. F. Root.	$0 75
The Culprit Fay.	J. L. Ensign.	1 00
The Twin Sisters.	H. G. Savoni.	50
Fairy Bridal.	Hewitt.	50
The Pic Nic.	J. R. Thomas.	1 00
Festival of the Rose.	J. C. Johnson.	30
Flower Festival on the Banks of the Rhine.	J. C. Johnson.	45
Spring Holiday.	C. C. Converse.	75
Quarrel Among the Flowers.	Shoeller.	35
Juvenile Oratorios. Containing "The Festival of the Rose," "The Indian Summer," and "The Children of Jerusalem." Three Cantatas. By	J. C. Johnson.	60

www.ingramcontent.com/pod-product-compliance
Lightning Source LLC
Chambersburg PA
CBHW020108170426
43199CB00009B/453